The Last
Democrat

The Last Democrat

edited by R. W. Bradford
with an introduction by Stephen Cox

Liberty Publishing
Port Townsend, Washington
1996

The essays in this book originally appeared, in different form, in *Liberty* magazine, except "Was the Pet Removed from the Premises?" which first appeared in *National Review* and is reprinted with permission of the authors.

SECOND PRINTING

ISBN 0-9638732-1-0

Liberty Publishing
P.O. Box 1181
Port Townsend, WA 98368

Printed in U.S.A.

Table of Contents

Preface
by R.W. Bradford

"Every decent man is ashamed of the government he lives under."
— *H.L. Mencken*

Bill Clinton has stolen from the public treasury, used his high office to attempt to coerce sexual favors from at least one employee, rewarded at least one sexual partner with a government job, used the FBI to investigate political opponents, trumped up criminal charges against a member of the White House staff to justify giving his job to a political ally, used the FBI to murder the members of a religious minority, and told more lies than he can count.

One might expect those who live under Bill Clinton's government would realize the truth of Mencken's dictum, and, bridling from shame, rush to join the campaign to prevent Clinton's re-election.

Well, count me out. Bill Clinton may be a scoundrel, a thief, a liar, and sexual predator, but he can scarcely disgrace the office of Richard Nixon, Ulysses S. Grant, and Lyndon Baines Johnson. Whoever replaces him will likely prove as much a scoundrel, thief, and liar as Clinton, but probably be a lot less amusing.

For the nation's political commentators and comedians, Bill Clinton's presidency is a gold mine. He combines the moralizing of Jimmy Carter and the womanizing of Jack Kennedy with the slipperiness of Ronald Reagan and the shiftiness of Richard Nixon. He can no more resist the abuse of power than he can resist a well-built woman or a super-size Coke to wash down his french fries and Big Mac. Like most successful American politicians, he has absolutely no moral sense yet exudes self-righteousness. Bill Clinton is a magnificent specimen of *Politicus americanus*.

But it is easy to fail to notice that beneath the stage from which buffoons like Clinton amuse us, there flow powerful historic currents. In the wake of the Great Depression, any attempt to swim against the tide of ever-expanding government would lead to death by drowning in the surf of public ridicule. Only a generation ago, the tide still seemed inexorable. Today that tide is ebbing. In 1994, a throng of opponents of big government was swept into office. Earlier this year, Bill Clinton himself admitted that "the era of big government is over." His problem now is that his party is a concatenation of special interests whose survival and prosperity depend on a perpetual increase in government power.

This book is both an exploration of these undercurrents and a celebration of the circus of American public life. The title essay argues that behind all the hoopla, something very important is happening: the notion that government is a magical entity that gives back more than it takes is dying, and the party that made that notion its creed is going down with it.

Bill Clinton's troubles are not the consequence of his dishonesty, his theft from the public treasury, his use of the FBI to investigate his political opponents, his persecuting the White House travel staff, his pervasive lying, or any of his other felonies, misdemeanors, and venial sins. His problem is that decades of increasing government power, higher taxes, and even higher spending have given us an out-of-control national debt, an insolvent Social Security system, an education system that doesn't educate, a growing underclass riven by violence and despair, and a diminishing productive class gradually becoming aware its their future is being sold to benefit a few coddled special interests, chief among them the officeholders of the Democratic Party.

Five months before the 1994 election, I wrote a commentary correctly predicting its outcome and prognosticating that Bill Clinton would be the last Democrat ever elected president. The title essay of this book grew out of that piece. The balance of the book offers a comprehensive examination of Bill Clinton: his character, ambitions, and career. Most of it was previously published in the pages of *Liberty*.

It goes without saying that an anthology of this sort is the work of many hands. In addition to those whose writing appears in these pages, I am indebted to *Liberty*'s editorial staff, especially to Timothy Virkkala, Jesse Walker, and Nathan Crow.

Port Townsend, Washington
June 1996

Introduction
by Stephen Cox

On the eve of the 1994 election, President Clinton, smiling his little Bobbsey-twin smile, went before a campaign audience and gave vent to some Arkansas folk wisdom. He was worried, he said, that people might fail to give him credit for the nation's "economic recovery." He did not mention the possibility that people might simply have missed this great event. If you were washing the dog or opening a can of soup, the "recovery" might easily have passed you unperceived.

Anyway, Clinton said that down in Arkansas there is a saying that if you're walking along the road and see a turtle on a fence post, you know that somebody put it there. What he seems to have meant was this: if a voter (i.e., a person walking along a road) sees evidence of an economic recovery (i.e., a turtle on a post), then the voter should conclude that somebody caused this recovery (i.e., put the turtle on the post), and that this somebody must be the president (i.e., himself).

Well, on the next day, election day, the president's folk metaphor really showed its mettle, though not in the way that he intended it to. The voters walked down the road, they saw a turtle on a fence post, they concluded that somebody had put the turtle there, and they knew that somebody must be Clinton. But the turtle they saw was an old, slow, one-eyed, hidebound, dirt-stained reptile with a nasty habit of biting any hand that dared to feed it. This turtle was nothing so wonderful as "economic recovery." It was the Democratic Party, the nation's loftiest and (arguably) most self-isolated political organism, protected and imprisoned by its dominance of Congress and the presidency.

This turtle had enjoyed its supreme position for two years, but now, sitting there on its fence post, it had no food, it had no water, and it was broiling in the embarrassing light of public scrutiny. This turtle couldn't even shit in private, and turtles shit a lot. Probably it just wanted to be left alone to waddle off and hide in some dim, nutrient swamp that only turtles know. But every time it looked down and wiggled its flippers as if to jump, it started getting dizzy. There were mean things down there, things that lay in wait for the turtle in case it ever lost its perch. There were investigations and indictments and trials; there was even the necessity of providing for itself, like all the other creatures in the swamp. So the turtle stayed where it was. It knew that Bill Clinton, in his single-minded pursuit of power, was responsible for its plight. He had put it there and left it there, where everyone could witness its double-dealing, double-talking, self-righteous, obscurantist misery.

When the voters saw all this, they knocked the turtle off its post.

Clinton lost the election, and he lost it on the old-fashioned collectivist program that wraps the Democratic Party like a hard, dull, dirty shell. He campaigned to the bitter end, and as he neared that end, he campaigned harder and more explicitly on the premise that government is good, and more government is better, because government does things for you that you couldn't conceivably do for yourself. The Republicans countered with the idea, largely borrowed from libertarians, that government should be limited. The Republicans were often lying about their allegiance to that idea. But the fact that they lied in this particular way simply enforces the point: the election was won by anti-collectivist sentiment.

The president himself claimed, on the morning after the election, that he had spent the last two years struggling for smaller government, which was what the voters had voted for, both when they elected him and when they elected his Republican enemies. Clinton's decision to run and cover from the pro-government campaign he had just conducted must have come hard. His new and outrageous claim, devised by the proposer of the largest peacetime takeover of the American economy, the "health care initiative," is further testimony to the power of the limited-government idea. Hypocrisy is the tribute that vice pays to virtue.

The collectivist defeat took a variety of concrete forms. Nationally, Republican victory in the House of Representatives put new and unexpected strength into the machinery of limited government, which depends on effective checks and balances. Because of this election, no one can take the inherited institutional authority of one party for granted any more. In local elections, voters showed renewed resistance to collectivist moral principles. Oregon passed an assisted-suicide initiative over the objections of people who argued that somebody besides the individual has the right to govern choices of life and death. In California, the Little Hillary initiative, a proposal to collectivize health insurance and subject it to the control of the state government, went down to ignominious defeat. Many states passed term limits proposals, which were carried against the opposition of people who believe that no limits should be placed on the power of majorities to make fools of themselves in perpetuity. The practical principle of republican government, as Madison argued, is limitation of the majority's power to do as it pleases.

In several localities, voters threw out Democratic grandees who had thriven for years on collectivization of money and influence, taking individuals' power and money and serving them back to the collective in the form of pork. Speaker of the House Foley ran for reelection solely on his ability to dole out pork to his district in eastern Washington. He lost his district. (Headline, front page, above the fold, *Los Angeles Times*, November 10, 1994: "With Foley, Noble Era Will End.") Senator Sasser of Tennessee and Governor Cuomo of New York — big taxers and bigger spenders — claimed that their three terms in office constituted an "investment," as Sasser said, that would in the very *next* term be returned to the people in a millennium of sufficient pork for every pot. Sasser and Cuomo lost their states.

Race-mongers, propagandizers for the most vicious form of collectivism, also lost. Mrs. Cuomo threatened that race riots would erupt if her husband were not reelected, but no one seemed to be listening. Opponents of California's Proposition 187, an attempt to deny welfare "rights" to illegal immigrants, merely damaged their cause by sending children into the streets to riot against the "racism" and "genocide" of the proposition. (As a libertarian, you may not be in favor of restrictions on immigration, but are you really in favor of inviting immigrants to come here by giving them welfare?) Nobody except Rush Limbaugh's audience seemed to care that Charles Rangel, who has represented a black district in Manhattan for about 1500 years, tried to convince people that a vote for tax cuts is actually a vote for "racism." The argument just didn't work any more.

To keep Rush's show amusing, God decided to spare a few of the most egregious Democrats from destruction. What would Rush, or any of us, do without Senator Kennedy — that enormous punching bag, chock-full of crap? While the senator was being reelected, several other Kennedys got elected or reelected to relatively minor offices, a development that may promise the rest of us some fun later on. Not that wickedness is confined to the Kennedys, or even to Democrats. A good number of evil and lunatic Republicans gained election, in some cases despite the electorate's full knowledge of their character. Again, a clear point is made: this election was about an issue, the power and loftiness of government. Whoever got on the wrong side of that issue was in danger; whoever got on the right side was not. All incumbent senators, representatives, and governors survived — so long as they were Republicans. And the Republicans survived and prospered because of their anti-government rhetoric.

Now, no one expects Republican legislators to live up to their rhetoric. Few of them, obviously, are dedicated to free-market classical liberalism. They are politicians, mostly small-town politicians, who are *infected* by classical liberal ideas — and, often enough, *confused* by them. The realignment of American politics that is now happening — typified by the desertion of Senator Shelby of Alabama from the Democrats to the Republicans — will have contradictory effects. The Democrats who survived the election are disproportionately representative of safe districts with far-left values. The Republicans who triumphed are mostly (a) safe-district conservatives full of down-home values, which are a mixed bag at best, and (b) committed ideologues who might never have achieved election in a normal year.

But if the Republicans want to keep winning, they might do well to think about the careers of such formerly marginal ideologues as Governor Engler of Michigan. A few months ago, Engler was considered a loser because he slashed welfare and destroyed the political influence of the public-school teachers' union, which was a mighty power in a union state. Engler stuck to his guns, refused to compromise, and won reelection by a big majority, meanwhile pulling a Republican candidate into the State Senate.

To make realignment work in their favor, Republicans need to study examples of success like that rather than the advice so eagerly offered by the political "experts" and the media. As soon as the shape of the election started to emerge on the evening of November 8, the experts were already offering the Republicans a stale concoction of "bipartisanship." William Schneider, who for some reason is CNN's political consultant, assured viewers that the "message" of the election was the need for bipartisanship. Other CNNers chimed in: "I'm not sure it's a mandate to move to the right; it's a mandate for action" — any kind of action, presumably, that would win bipartisan approval.

The cry, or whimper, was taken up by the Democrats. Cuomo, that unyielding partisan of modern liberalism, assured everyone that "partisanship for its own sake is a waste of time." Senator Robb of Virginia, who threw everything but the kitchen sink at his Republican opponent, said that the election "will force us to work together." Clinton thought he heard the people "demand[ing] that a more equally divided [!] Congress work together with the president." The point of this pishposh was to spread responsibility wherever it could possibly be spread, so that the Democratic elite would never again have to sit on that fence post and endure that sun.

Clinton, of course, always tries to diffuse responsibility until there's not a smidgen of it left. In his post-election press conference, he offered to take his "share of responsibility" for the Democrats' shell-shattering fall, but he had awful trouble with the word "I." "We," he said, "made mistakes in government, but I'm proud of the things we've been able to accomplish together."

The Republicans must make sure that Clinton's "together" doesn't include them.

The Last Democrat
by R. W. Bradford

Bill Clinton will be the last elected Democratic president for a long time — probably the last ever. As the political home of an archaic tax-and-spend philosophy, the Democratic Party is simply obsolescent, as obsolescent as the Whig Party in the 1850s or the Soviet Communist Party in 1989. The party that began with the election of Thomas Jefferson in 1800 may well end with the defeat of William Jefferson Clinton in 1996, or with his leaving office in disgrace.

Clinton's personal corruption and his failure to enact his legislative program are symptoms of his party's collapse, but they are not the underlying cause. As the twentieth century ends, America is on the verge of a fundamental change in its political culture. Stripped to its essence, politics in America from the 1920s to the 1990s was the application of a rather simple recipe, first formulated by Franklin Roosevelt's welfare boss, Harry Hopkins: tax and tax, spend and spend, elect and elect. The recipe worked because Americans believed that government is a magical entity that can take money from all of us and give back more than it took, making us all richer in the process.*

This faith underlies all sorts of government policy, from subsidies to farmers to "free" college tuition to Social Security to deficit spending to the Great Society to military adventures overseas. It dominated American political culture while most of us grew up, so powerfully and so totally that it needed no name. It just passed as common belief. But it went by many names: modern liberalism, left-liberalism, the middle of the road. It has been tempered only by the American tradition of an open society, which provided limited protection for freedom of speech

---

* Stated baldly like that, this theory seems crazy. But it was seldom stated baldly.

and religion.

And it set an agenda for American politics that never varied. The Democrats proposed bigger programs, more powerful government, and higher taxes; the Republicans responded by proposing to expand the power of government at a more moderate pace.

When I call this belief-system a "faith," I mean exactly that. Rooseveltian liberalism took on the trappings of a civic religion, with its own rituals and dogmas. There is the ritual of voting, based on the bizarre belief that one ballot in a national election can make a difference in the outcome. There is the dogma of the "mandate," in which whoever wins — no matter how narrow the margin, no matter how low the turnout — is said to have been given a mandate by the voters to enact his agenda. There is the deification of the leader, represented by the odd but persistent hope that if we only elect the right man, he will solve our problems for us.

Above all, there are the mysteries and sacraments of the redistributive state. The poor, we are told, will be supported by government welfare programs, financed by taxes on the rich and the middle class. The middle class will be assisted by Social Security, Medicare, student loans, and the like — all financed by taxes on the poor and working class. The rich will enjoy a vast array of corporate subsidies and loopholes, paid for by everyone who is not rich and quite a few who are. Farmers will be paid to grow crops, and also *not* to grow crops. When this raises food prices, the very poor will be given vouchers so they can afford to eat — vouchers financed, in large part, by the merely *somewhat* poor. Wages and profits will be "protected" by tariff barriers — barriers that raise the cost of living for everyone, whether or not they are "protected."

Supposedly, all this will benefit every American, and not just those people best positioned to take advantage of the political process. This article of faith is truly more mysterious, its logic more occult, than any belief any traditional religion may preach.

There were dissenters, of course. There were the totalitarians, who took faith in government to its logical extreme, arguing that the state should completely control the economic, social, and even personal lives of the people. During the early years of the Welfare State Era, totalitarian dissent came from both the Left and the Right. The left-totalitarians were in league with the Soviet Union, the right-totalitarians with Nazi Germany. World War II pretty well wiped out the totalitarian Right in this country, but the totalitarian Left continued to prosper until the collapse of its sponsor.

There was also dissent from another direction, from people who altogether rejected faith in government as a magical institution. Some of these dissenters considered themselves a remnant of the previous liberal social order. Others considered themselves prophets of a new, even freer social order. But these old-fashioned liberals, libertarians, and anarchists were few and unorganized. All were profoundly alienated from a society that considered their views reactionary, lunatic, or irrelevant.

For a while, the theory of government as magical institution seemed to work. The twentieth century was the American Century. As Europe fought two bloody and almost incalculably expensive world wars and a third of the world's population fell under the control of a psychotic and reactionary Communist system, the U.S. became the richest country on Earth.

Then Communism failed, and Europe and Japan emerged from their wars with freer economies than before. Gradually, they caught up with and surpassed the U.S.

During the last few years, Americans have begun to lose their faith in the magical power of government. Despite almost universal opposition from the media, politicians of both parties, and entrenched government bureaucracies, voters in numerous states passed term limitation measures. In the 1990 congressional elections, the vote for the anti-government Libertarian Party *doubled.* In 1992, H. Ross Perot came out of nowhere to get 19% of the presidential vote, enabling Clinton to squeak into office with a bare plurality of 43%.

In 1988, it was widely and accurately observed that an incumbent member of Congress had a better chance of being re-elected than an incumbent member of the Soviet Politburo. It's easy to see why: congressmen had voted themselves huge powers to reward their constituents with spending bills, built up huge staffs to perform "constituent services," acquired tremendous government-subsidized campaigning privileges, and taken in huge amounts of "contributions" from special interests groups. But in 1992, things were different: 122 congresspeople lost their re-election bids or retired. (The retirement rate was extraordinarily high, thanks to two factors: many congresspeople were under fire for corruption and decided that discretion was the better form of valor, and a law was about to take effect that would prohibit retiring congresspeople from pocketing for personal use campaign funds extorted from lobbyists and special interests.)

Bill Clinton interpreted his 43% as a mandate and immediately set about promoting a traditional Democratic program. He sought to fight crime by pouring $30 billion into midnight basketball leagues, adding 100,000 new cops to the streets of American cities, and preventing private citizens from owning guns for self-defense. He sought to reduce the deficit by raising taxes. He appointed aggressive regulators to head federal agencies. He addressed rising health-care costs by proposing the government take over the entire industry, lock, stock, and barrel.

But it didn't work. By returning to the old welfare state agenda of higher taxes, more regulation, and gigantic, elaborate government programs, Clinton focused the voters' attention on the failures of their old faith.

The results were predictable. Everywhere, energized anti-government conservatives sought Republican nominations for elective office. Almost everywhere, elected Democrats tried to downplay their records. They omitted the word "Democrat" from their advertising, claimed to favor downsizing government, claimed to be trying to balance the budget. In my state, the only political advertisement I saw that could even remotely be described as favoring the welfare state was a pro–Social Security ad by the incumbent Republican senator.

It was on September 26, 1994 that the Democrats' political doom was finally laid out for everyone to see. That was the day then–Senate Majority Leader George Mitchell admitted that health care "reform" was dead.

The Clintons claimed it was the partisanship of the Republicans and special interests that defeated their scheme, but they couldn't be more wrong. The Republicans hardly even opposed his plan; instead, they proposed more "moderate" versions of the program. They stood up against it only after the people made it clear that they didn't want it. (I was reminded of something columnist Tom Anderson said back in the 1960s: "Democrats want to move to socialism at 100 miles an hour. Republicans only want to socialize at 50 miles per hour.") And the program was defeated by the exact opposite of special interests: the general interest of all Americans. It took time, but people came to realize that Clinton's program would cause either health care rationing or escalating taxes, or (more likely) both. The Republicans finally noticed that the people didn't buy the scheme, so they stopped proposing watered-down versions and began to oppose it.

The voters simply weren't supporting Rooseveltian liberalism anymore.

Clinton clearly didn't understand what was happening. After watching his popularity drop in the polls all year, he tried the oldest trick in the book: invade a tiny country, then go on a triumphant tour of the world.* Sure enough, this boosted his popularity, to the point where almost half the American people thought maybe he wasn't doing such a bad job.

But then he made a mistake. He came home and decided to hit the campaign trail on behalf of his fellow Democrats. He traipsed from one end of the country to the other like a political Joe Blfstk, spreading disaster wherever he went. Everywhere he visited, his fellow Democrats fell in the polls. He destroyed the campaigns of Democratic Senate candidates in Michigan, Washington, Minnesota, and Pennsylvania. Of 21 Democrat-held Senate seats up for election, the Republicans won eight. Every Republican-held seat stayed Republican. Of 278 seats in the House held by Democrats, Republicans captured 56, ousting 33 incumbents in the process. Prominent Democratic casualties included House Speaker Tom Foley, indicted Ways and Means Chairman Dan Rostenkowski, and Judiciary Chairman Jack Brooks.

Republicans won virtually every campaign they seriously contested. The exceptions merely illustrated their strength, though not always their sense. In Virginia, the party lost when they nominated a convicted perjurer and the party's senior elected official sponsored an "independent" candidacy by another Republican to split the GOP vote. In California, their nominee was an airhead who spent $26 million of his inheritance on his campaign but never figured out where he stood on the issues and was caught in a blatant act of hypocrisy. Even so, nei-

---

* On August 25, 1994, President Clinton's crime bill was passed, thanks to a last-minute decision by several members of the House Black Caucus to forsake their opposition and cast their lot with the president. Twenty-five days later, the United States sent an army of occupation to Haiti, thanks to a last-minute decision by Bill Clinton to forsake his opposition and follow the policy recommendation of the Black Caucus. It makes one wonder: if the president's crime bill had passed easily, without needing the support of the Black Caucus, would the Marines have found themselves shooting Haitians? I know Clinton promised us more cops on the street, but I assumed he meant *in this country*.

ther incumbent Democratic senator managed to get half the popular vote.

The president's spin doctors went to work, claiming that the voters were just expressing anti-Congress feelings. The trouble with this theory is that Clinton's fellow Democrats did even worse running for governor than they did running for Congress, winning just nine of 31 races and losing the governorship of every large state except Florida. The spin doctors also tried claiming that the voters weren't rejecting Clinton or his policies; they were just rejecting incumbents. The problem with this theory is that every single Republican incumbent in the House, the Senate, and the governors' mansions was re-elected. The salient characteristic of the Republican victory was its pervasiveness. Republicans gained control of both houses of Congress, most governorships, and many state legislatures. The last time the United States had seen anything like this was in 1930, when the Depression converted the Republicans from the natural majority party everywhere but the South into what seemed like a permanent minority.

Today, the Democrats are in virtually the same condition the Republicans were in 1930. They still control the presidency, and they still have a few small constituencies that will give them their die-hard support. But their day is through.

This book tries to explain why their day is through. It explores the Clintons' big-government agenda, explaining not only why it must fail as *policy*, but why it is now failing as *politics*. It examines the corruption of the Clintons and their cronies, detailing not just *how* they have looted the public treasury, but *why* the power left-liberalism vests in government makes such corruption inevitable. It takes a close look at the holocaust at Waco, showing how it illustrates the moral bankruptcy of modern liberalism, its decline from lofty aspirations of social justice and tolerance to vicious repression and mass murder.

When Bill Clinton told a reporter that her question about his tax returns was the sort of thing that causes "a dangerous public cynicism about government," he was doing more than trying to hide his corrupt activities. He was defending the new religion of the modern world, the deep-rooted faith in government. And his warning was on target. The exposure of corruption — whether of Richard Nixon, the Clintons, Lyndon Johnson, Boris Yeltsin, or Fidel Castro — eats away at people's faith in government as a miracle-working institution capable of creating paradise on Earth, staffed by saints selflessly dedicated to the common good.

That faith is failing. And that is why Clinton is the Last Democrat.

Presidential Malpractice
by R. W. Bradford

I just got back from my dentist's, where I had my regular check-up. Five x-rays, a cleaning by a dental hygienist, and a brief examination set me back $117. A year ago, this same procedure cost me $97. Five years ago it cost less than $60.

It's a good thing I didn't have to have anything *done* to my teeth. Being healthy is expensive enough.

My experience typifies that of all Americans. Medical costs are rising rapidly, much more rapidly than other prices. Over the last decade, national health care expenditures have risen at more than twice the rate of inflation, from 9.4% of GNP in 1980 to over 12.8% of GNP in 1994. In my home state of Washington, spending on medical care rose 153% over the course of the '80s. Total national health expenditures have increased from $27.1 billion in 1960, to $250.1 billion in 1980, to $666.2 billion in 1990. All facets of the health care industry are seeing costs rise faster than the general inflation rate — hospital care, physician services, dental services, home health care, drug prices, the whole array. The average cost of medical coverage has also risen, especially in the last few years: from $1,645 per person in 1984 to $3,968 in 1992.

The trend is plain to see. If the price of medical services continues to rise at this rate, Americans will be bankrupted or have to forgo needed care. This is why so many Americans responded to President Clinton's call for "health care reform."

Like a megalomaniacal Santa Claus, stymied by a Congress that recognized porkbarrel when it saw it, Bill Clinton focused his attention on medical care after his "economic stimulus" package was eviscerated by Congress. "The only thing we'll really have to give the American people is health care," he confided to one government official. And so it came to pass that Clinton chose to make his health care plan the central achievement of his presidency, the crowning glory that would buy him a place in history and popularity sufficient for re-election, perhaps this time with a majority of the popular vote.

Taking the Task Force to Task

But the "reforms" Clinton offered us were worse than the problem itself. The very way in which his health plan was devised should be a tip-off. Virtually his first act as president was to appoint a health reform task force of "experts" to study the situation. To protect it from undue influence from those with a financial interest in medical care (i.e., health care professionals), he kept the membership of the task force secret and instructed it to meet in private.

Unhappily for the president, on March 10, 1993, Federal Judge Royce Lambeth ruled that it was illegal for the task force to meet in total secrecy so long as the president's wife headed it without pay. Presidential spin doctor George Stephanopoulos immediately went on television and explained with a straight face that the court's decision was a "victory" for the administration because it did not disband the task force altogether.

Eventually, someone leaked a list of the members to the press and to Congress. On March 28, it apparently occurred to the president (or his wife) that since Judge Lambeth had ordered it to hold public meetings, people were going to figure out who was on it anyway, so they might as well come clean.

It turned out that the task force had 511 members, of whom 412 were full-time employees of the federal government. Another 82 were part-time federal government employees. This left 17 who were not federal bureaucrats. Of these 17, nine were employees of the National Governors' Association, six were consultants for the Department of Health and Human Services, one was a county commissioner, and one was affiliated with the Harvard Community Health Association.

It's a safe bet that a task force consisting of government

employees will conclude that medical care ought to be controlled even more tightly by government than it is today.

During the eight months of its existence, Ms. Clinton's group released statements and "leaks" revealing a vision that developed and grew. At first, it proposed a simple expansion of the current private-government partnership that has resulted in ever-increasing medical costs. By steps large and small, it progressed toward its final proposal: the cartelization of medical care in government-sponsored oligopolies — socialized medicine in all but name.

But the discussion and evolution of the task force's thinking was a sham for public consumption. In fact, Mr. and Mrs. Clinton had devised their health care plan even before they took office in January. Indeed, by February 1992, almost a year before taking office, Clinton agreed to put Ira Magaziner in charge of medical care reform because he knew that Magaziner's thinking in favor of mandatory universal "insurance" managed by government-organized cartels was "in sync" with his own. "By the time [President Clinton] talked to me about the job," HHS Secretary Donna Shalala said, "he was already clear on what he wanted to do and how. . . . It was pretty much ruffles and flourishes after that. . ."

While the task force was leaking proposals that it was pretending to consider and the press was full of speculation about the secret membership of the task force, Magaziner was given power to control virtually everything the task force did. "Mr. Magaziner alone decided what numbers to crunch and when," *The Wall Street Journal* reported, "and only he was allowed to see everything." Not surprisingly, the task force ended up recommending exactly what Clinton and Magaziner had decided on more than a year earlier. Under the plan, employers would be required to buy comprehensive health care packages for their employees from large health care cartels, called "regional alliances." These cartels would spend money in compliance with budgets set by the National Health Board, which would be appointed by the president. By controlling how every dollar is spent, the cartels would determine what doctors and medical researchers do. They would control also what medical care each American would receive and from whom each of us would receive it.

The only issues the task force (and the president's advisors) were left to wrestle with were public relations and funding. The public relations effort went very well. One day Mr. or Mrs. Clinton promised new benefits to the public without cost, the next day some tragic story was told about how some uninsured or underinsured family had serious problems paying for their medical care — all against a backdrop of television commercials advising us that the solution is "managed care" and pontificating professors explaining why we need more government control. A parade of "victims" came to Washington to appear before television cameras. Typical was the family of an infant poisoned by the *E. coli* bacterium; the parents testified about the importance of a government takeover of the health care industry. Since the child was recovering and his medical bills were paid by those responsible for his accidental poisoning, the relevance of this testimony was more than a little shaky, but matters of logic and relevance never get in the way of political rhetoric. The campaign for a "solution" seemed to infect virtually every newscast and public affairs program.

The only pothole on the road was money. Obviously, extending medical insurance to 37 million Americans and expanding it for millions more was going to cost a lot. So every once in a while, Ms. Clinton paused in her public listing of new benefits and attacks on red tape to mention the matter of paying for the program. At first, she said health care reform could be accomplished by mandatory private insurance for all but the unemployed, for whom government would pick up the tab. This wasn't terribly popular — people began to suspect that they would have to pay for their own insurance, which already costs too much. So the task force suggested financing it like Social Security. But this meant lower take-home pay for everyone. So the task force floated the idea of a value added tax. But taxes seem high enough to most people already, and the VAT would fall hardest on the poor. So Ms. Clinton proposed a "progressive" tax requiring people with high incomes to pay far more than those with lower incomes for identical health care. Even this failed to gain much support from a public worried about higher taxes.

The problem the task force faced was simple and fundamental. Americans have a system of extensive and wonderful benefits and services, delivered to them with little hassle or worry. But they do not want to pay for it, though they don't mind *someone else* paying. The problem is that the benefits Ms. Clinton promised are expensive. They cannot be paid for simply by raising taxes on the wealthy or some other small minority.

Every time the president's wife or one of her staff floated the notion of a new tax, support for the whole program receded. It was not until August that the task force came up with an approach that worked: simply tell the American public that the system won't require *anyone* to pay for it, except for cigarette smokers and profiteering price-gougers.

In sum, the high-profile task force appointed to investigate the health care crisis and develop solutions was a fraud. It was not engaged in investigation and the only thing it proposed was a plan that had already been decided upon by the president and his wife. At a cost to taxpayers of millions of dollars, the task force engaged in an elaborate charade for the sole purpose of selling the public on the Clintons' proposal.

The Clintons' plan dutifully endorsed by the task force called for expanded benefits at virtually no cost. Everyone would have been covered, even if they were unemployed or work for a firm that cannot afford to pay for the mandated program. And the benefits to those already insured by the government would have been greatly expanded. At present, those covered by government medical care programs are not covered if they retire early. Nor are their prescription drugs paid for. Nor is long-term hospitalization. Under the Clintons' proposal, medical care during early retirement, prescription drugs, and long-term hospitalization would have been guaranteed to all Americans. These are all very popular and extremely expensive.

How would all this be paid for?

According to the Clintons, extending insurance to 37 million uninsured Americans and expanding the coverage of the insurance of the other 220 million Americans could have been paid for by increasing cigarette taxes and squeezing $285 billion of waste out of the medical care programs the government already runs. The bottom line for most Americans, Clinton argued time after time, is that they would get more and pay less.

But one group of Americans would have been destined to get much less and pay a lot more: employees of major companies. Under the present system, many major firms have agreed to pay virtually all the costs of medical care for their employees and their employees' families. The uncontrollably rising cost of this "fringe benefit" threatens the profitability and even the viability of many large businesses. By proposing to legislate an end to these contractual obligations, the Clintons provided a powerful incentive for big business to support their plan. Indeed, *The Wall Street Journal* figures that big businesses would have been able to pocket 20% to 30% of the funds they have set aside to provide future medical care for employees.

Most initial opposition to the Clinton plan came from smaller businesses, who generally do not provide medical care as a fringe benefit. Paying 7.9% of wages for health care may seem like a bargain for a big corporation that currently pays 15%, but it seems pretty expensive for small businesses that currently provide no health care benefits at all. To try to reduce the opposition of small businesses, the Clintons proposed an outright subsidy that would provide coverage to their employees for a tiny fraction of the price big businesses will pay.

There is a strong possibility that the new subsidy would have proven ephemeral: as expenses for the program rise and the public clamors for cutting costs and closing loopholes, it would become a likely target for elimination.

And even if it did survive, it would not make up for another blow to small business embedded in the Clinton plan. I refer to the provisions for enterprises that try to reclassify employees as "independent contractors" in order to avoid the tax liability for their medical care. To prevent this form of tax minimization, the Clintons' legislation granted the IRS broad powers to define who is and who is not an independent contractor. At first inspection, this may sound like a pretty minor change in the law. But it's not.

Like most definitional issues, the question of whether a person is an employee or an independent contractor has long been a confusing and convoluted matter. After years of expensive argument and litigation, Congress simplified the matter by enacting "safe harbor" provisions in the Revenue Act of 1978. Under this law, if the common practice of an industry is to treat workers as independent contractors, the IRS is to treat them as independent contractors. If the Clintons' medical care legislation had been enacted, that "safe harbor" would have been abolished, the IRS will be able to reclassify virtually any independent contractor as an employee, and businesses will have no alternative but to negotiate, appeal, and litigate.

That didn't get much play in the press, of course. But then, with a plan this big, it's almost impossible for most busy reporters to keep up with all that's in it, or to reason out all the implications of what they do know. This made the media unhappily susceptible to even more government manipulation than usual, with White House players setting the agenda for most coverage of the debate.

It is worth noting that it was not until October 28, 1993 — some 281 days after formally promising Americans "health care reform" — that Bill Clinton confessed that his plan would increase the cost of medical care for some 40% of all Americans, and that he released this information, not in one of his nationally telecast addresses to the American people or an appearance on *Larry King Live* or any of his wife's high-profile appearances, but in the obscure congressional testimony of one of his minions.

How many times during those 281 days did Bill Clinton, Hillary Rodham Clinton, or one of their subordinates explain how much money the program would "save"? how much "wasteful red tape" would be "eliminated"? how it would eliminate "duplication of services"? and "bureaucracy and paperwork"?

Not surprisingly, most Americans made the logical inference that after savings of only-God-knows-how-many billions of dollars each year, the cost of health care would go down for virtually everyone. Then it turned out that for more than 100,000,000 Americans, the cost would increase, if the administration's quietly admitted estimate of October 28 is accurate. But then, why should this figure have any credibility, coming as it did after 281 days of intensive P.R. (i.e. lies) designed to convince people that almost everyone's medical costs would go down?

The Ugly Truth About the President's Program

Throughout the debate, Clinton and his expert commission dodged the nastiest question that perplexes every system of socialized medicine: triage administration — i.e., the government deciding which people's medical problems ought not be treated at all. Triage is inherent to the Clinton program, though its advocates often refuse to admit it, and those who do prefer to call it "rationing."

Unless an infinite amount of resources is allocated to health care, someone has to decide which medical problems will be treated. In a free market, those allocations are made on the basis of willingness and ability to pay. This means that some serious medical problems of poor people will not be treated, and that some rather fanciful problems of the wealthy will. To many, this is simply unjust. Why should a poor man die because he cannot afford an appendectomy, while a rich woman can have extract of sheep embryo injected into her blood on the theory that it will make her younger?

Those who find this situation unsatisfactory seldom talk about the alternative, perhaps because it isn't much more pleasant. If decisions about how money is to be spent for health care are not to be made by individuals themselves, then who *is* to make the decision?

One possible answer is that the individual can purchase insurance. In exchange for a fee, the insurance company agrees to provide such medical care as an individual needs. The care the insurance company will provide (or pay for) is determined by what the insurance buyer contracts for. If one buys insurance that covers dental care, the insurer pays one's dental bills; if one has not contracted for dental care, then he is responsible for paying for it himself. So ultimately, voluntary insurance does not change the method of allocation: whether it is a poor person buying insurance against appendicitis or a wealthy person buying insurance to pay for rejuvenation injections doesn't matter. They get what they pay for.

The only alternative to allocating medical care by means of the ability and willingness of the individual to pay for it is allocation by a third party. That third party — whether an individual or a committee — must decide whether to pay for a medical procedure. Ultimately, that third party will have the power of life or death.

This has been the experience of every country that has adopted government-allocated medical care. This triage is sometimes obscured. In Britain, for example, those who are wealthy enough can purchase medical care that the National Health Service refuses to pay for. Canada denies its wealthy this same privilege — it is against the law to contract with a physician to provide medical care not provided by the national health insurance program. But this is softened by the proximity of the United States, where private health care is widely available.

Of course, Clinton and his experts do not mention any of this. Instead they focus on a single point: the present system is so expensive that some people might not be able to afford the care that they want or need. They promise a new system that will provide what people want at low cost, or at no cost at all.

The president's proposal empowered his National Health Board to control costs. This would have been a tall order. All human experience suggests that government control raises costs, thanks to its inherent inflexibility, inefficiency, and waste. As spending spirals, the pressure to control costs will mount. And there are only two ways that the centralized medical bureaucracy can control costs: by limiting medical research and by limiting what diseases and injuries will be treated and which patients will get care.

Faced with a choice between triage and research cuts, the National Health Board would almost certainly cut research. Triage has very visible victims, people who can appear on television and tell their sad tale of how they are denied medical care. People who die because research was discontinued or mismanaged by the government are not so visible as victims of triage. And medical progress would continue for a while, thanks to research already well underway or completed but not yet available to consumers. The time lapse while progress slows down would obscure the fact that it resulted from Clinton's program.

But triage would still be inevitable, for costs will rise inexorably under a system offering universal health care at no direct cost to the consumer, even after research is eliminated. And it would come gradually, as it has in other countries with similar systems. In Britain, for example, people over 65 are frequently denied treatment; in general, in nations with socialized medicine, the elderly are the first to be denied care when resources become too scarce. British citizens are regularly denied life-saving treatment: every year, around 9,000 British kidney patients are refused renal dialysis or a needed transplant, and as many as 15,000 people with cancer and 17,000 heart patients cannot get the treatment they need. Canadian patients often have to wait months for treatment that would be available within days in the relatively freer medical markets of the United States.

Sometimes the rationing falls along racial lines. In Canada, despite the surface shimmer of political correctness, minorities nonetheless find themselves on the losing end of medical rationing: studies of Inuit and Cree people in northern Quebec demonstrate lower access to health care, lower life expectancy, and higher infant mortality rates for those groups.

The *reductio ad absurdum* of centralized triage administration was reached when Canadians discovered that dogs were getting CAT scans faster than people were. It is illegal in Canada to pay extra money for more immediate treatment, but there was no law prohibiting pet owners for paying extra to get quick CAT scans for their dogs, and hospitals could see no reason why their equipment should not be used during off-hours to raise funds for needed improvements. As a result, rich canines could get services for which ordinary people had to queue up for months.

Did the Canadian authorities, when this story was reported, allow people the same right dogs had? Of course not. They simply extended human restrictions to cover dogs as well. Now *no one* gets after-hours CAT scans, and the hospital must get by without the additional funding.

All this is not to say the widespread denial of needed medical care would have begun as soon as the Clinton program was enacted. There is always a gap between the implementation of a policy and its consequences. The implementation of Medicare and Medicaid in the mid-1960s made government the biggest force in the medical care industry and led inevitably to massive waste; costs spiralled out of control. But it took a quarter century for the mounting waste and costs to become evident to most people. During much of that period, it seemed like the laws of economics had been repealed. Americans enjoyed what they always liked to call "the best health care system in the world": extensive care available at practically no cost to practically everyone.

Though not immediate, the results were indeed inevitable. When the consequences of the first major government incursion into health care finally became evident, the advocates of government intervention proposed yet another incursion as the solution. The Clinton program ultimately would have made the situation worse. But, as in the '60s, it would buy time. Once again, for a while it would appear that the program was working. Eventually, medical research would come to a near-halt and triage would be widespread. By the time this next "crisis" hit, advocates of government expansion would no doubt propose yet another "solution."

Big Brother Is Watching You

There is one more way in which the government would attempt to control costs in a socialized or cartelized system. Every American's leisure activities, eating habits, sleep patterns, entertainment preferences — ultimately, every activity a person engages in — has an effect on one's health. If the cost of medical care is paid by the government, the government will have a legitimate interest in regulating or prohibiting activities that harm one's health — all in the name of "controlling costs."

Do you ski? Well, if the government is going to pay to haul you to the hospital, set your broken bones, and provide you with physical rehabilitation, then it has a vital interest in minimizing your risk of injury. Indeed, an activity as dangerous as skiing might best be made illegal altogether.

Do you eat French food? C'mon, everyone knows that stuff is high in cholesterol. Should you be allowed to eat it if I have to pick up the tab for your open-heart surgery?

Do you get a full eight hours of sleep every night? No? Well, you're inviting all sorts of health problems, and it isn't fair to make me and others (who all get *our* full eight hours) pay for your refusal to have good personal habits.

Do you engage in sex? Everyone knows that diseases are sometimes spread by sexual intercourse. And for women, sex is a notorious way of getting pregnant, complications of which (e.g., giving birth) can be very expensive.

The logic here is precisely the logic that subject all colleges and universities to federal regulation: so long as the government provides loans or aid to so much as a single student, the government has a right to regulate. The same logic justifies the requirement that building contractors doing government work follow certain business practices (e.g., pay prevailing union wages), and a million other impositions of regulations.

So anyone who supports a government takeover of medicine should think real hard about whether he or she wants the government regulating every aspect of his or her private life.

If you think this is alarmist, think again. Even without fully socialized medicine, the same argument has often been used very effectively to diminish personal freedom. Consider the debate about mandatory helmets for motorcyclists. In every state where these laws have been considered someone raises the point that while not wearing a motorcycle helmet may indeed be dangerous, it is dangerous only to the person who does not wear the helmet, so what business is it of the government anyway? And in every case, someone points out that some of the motorcyclists who get head injuries from accidents are taken to public hospitals for medical care and cannot pay their bills, thereby costing the taxpayer money.*

Indeed, the implication that government ought to outlaw unhealthy behavior or mandate healthy behavior was included in the public discussion of the bill. It provided the logic for imposing a tax on cigarette smokers of 3.75¢ per cigarette that they purchase. Cigarette smokers should pay more, it was argued, because they willfully engage in an unhealthy habit which increases the cost of providing them medical care. (Curiously, most people seem to accept this argument at face value, without any empirical verification. Has anyone researched the cost of treating cigarette smokers versus the cost of treating nonsmokers? It seems to me that most of the diseases consequent of cigarette-smoking strike at an earlier age than the diseases of nonsmokers, are very often relatively cheap to treat, and shorten the length of time that medical care must be paid for: cigarette smokers tend to die in their 60s or early 70s of inoperable cancer, instead of lingering into decrepitude and a need for long-term care.)

Of course, what would happen under government-run medicine would not be so rational as I suggest. The unhealthy habits of minorities would be proscribed, but the unhealthy habits of the majority would not, for the same reason that imbibing alcohol is legal and smoking *Cannabis sativa* is a felony, despite the fact that alcohol is linked to hundreds of thousands of illnesses and deaths each year, while marijuana is practically benign. Or the same reason that motorcyclists must wear helmets and the occupants of automobiles do not, even though wearing full-faced helmets would cut the rate of injuries to automobile occupants as surely as doing so cuts injuries to motorcyclists. Or that selling

---

* In June 1996, the governor of the state of Washington, which had enacted its own somewhat less opprobrious form of the Clintons' health care scheme, proposed additional laws against cigarette smoking on the grounds that every time a cigarette smoker lights up he is placing an unfair burden on the taxpayer who must ultimately pay for the smoker's bad habits.

crack cocaine is subject to much greater penalties than selling powdered cocaine — the effect on health is the same, but crack is customarily sold by African-Americans, powder by white guys. For that matter, the rank discrimination and punishment meted out to cigarette smokers is surely more a matter of their minority status and powerlessness than of any objective costs the government bears for their habit.

So it is more reasonable to expect that heterosexual relations between man and wife will not be restricted, but other forms will, despite the fact that the cost to the public treasury of pregnancy and birth will be far greater than the cost of treating sexually transmitted diseases.

The logic of the welfare state has already done away with the notion that any economic activity is genuinely private and therefore not subject to government regulation. If the Clintons had gotten their way, the idea that personal habits are private and therefore exempt from government regulation would have died as well.

Goodbye, Privacy

But the Clinton plan's threat to civil liberties went much deeper than that. One police-state measure would have gone into effect as soon as the White House's proposal became law.

I refer to the provision that everyone covered by the program — that is to say, everyone in the country — be required to carry an identity card containing a computer-readable record of all aspects of his or her medical history. In order to achieve this, the National Health Board would "enforce unique identification numbers for consumers." All Americans would have been required to carry the card with them at all times. It seems clear that anyone with the properly programmed credit card reader who got hold of your card could acquire all the details of your medical history — including any history of past psychological counseling, abortions, sexually transmitted diseases, alcoholism, or other information you consider to be highly private.

Which raises the question: what will stop a prospective employer or granter of credit from demanding your card and reviewing your medical history? The Clinton proposal said the data would be protected by "national security safeguards" and open only to "authorized persons, for authorized purposes, at authorized times." But these can be pretty thin protections. It seems that everyone from my insurance company to the university I attended has wanted my Social Security number, and on more than one occasion I have attempted to invoke the federal law that restricts the use of my Social Security number to taxpayer identification and Social Security business. In a few cases, these busybodies have complied, if only after putting me through a fair amount of trouble. ("No one's ever made this request before. You'll have to see Mr. So-and-So about this. I think he'll be back next week, but check with his secretary. In the meantime, I am not authorized to issue you a library card.") Usually, the response is, "Well, you don't *have* to give us your number. But we don't *have* to admit you to this university."

Furthermore, your medical data would be backed up in a huge national database. Once again, access to it would be protected by "national security safeguards" and open only to "authorized persons, for authorized purposes, at authorized times." Which means that someone wanting it would have to make a small bribe to an official of one of the bureaus that has "authorized" access to it, just as today private detectives routinely get information from "private" tax returns.

And once a uniform national identity card is mandated for all Americans, what are the chances it will not be used for other purposes as well? Like police data? Or information on how often you leave the country? Or a record of how current your tax payments are? Or any information about you that any government bureau believes it should maintain?

A similar proposal for a national identification card was

floated by the Reagan administration as an immigration measure. It was killed largely by the efforts of Martin Anderson, then an advisor to the president. Anderson later carried on a one-man crusade against Clinton's I.D. card in his syndicated column. But in the morass of seemingly larger issues, this one was largely overlooked.

Conservatives Dodge the Issue

You might expect political conservatives, the avowed advocates of individual responsibility, free markets, and sound economics, to lead opposition to the program by pointing out its obvious flaws. But with a few notable exceptions, conservatives first responded with obfuscation and compromise.

At first, the Right busied itself denying that any problem exists at all. Then, as it became evident that the public was not happy with the current situation and wanted some kind of reform, they withdrew from the issue.

Consider Fred Barnes' essay "What Health-Care Crisis?" in the May 1993 *American Spectator*. Barnes made some valid points: the uninsured do receive medical treatment, many statistics that are supposed to indict American health care in fact reflect other social problems, and socialized medicine would create more problems than it would solve.

But his major thesis was that American medicine is not in trouble because the American health care system is better than that of any other nation in the world. The only problem Barnes conceded is "lack of proper primary care for several million Americans." Nowhere does he address the issues of rising costs or government intervention. Why should we worry about rising costs, he seemed to be saying, since costs are rising even faster elsewhere? But the fact that Japan, Germany, Canada, et al. have worse problems than we do hardly indicates that our system is working fine.

Other conservatives offered even weaker arguments. Take

Donald Lambro, who spent his syndicated column of April 5, 1993 denouncing medical price controls and praising the "extraordinary advances" in "new surgical procedures and miraculous drugs" that are "saving more lives, extending longevity, and, yes, substantially cutting health care costs."

Lambro, like Barnes, missed the point. For one thing, it is doubtful that new technology is reducing health care costs; often, new technologies are more expensive, as well as more effective, than those they replace. But even to the dubious extent that technological advances cut costs, their effect is limited. A television costs more than a radio — but is cheaper for what it provides. Progress brings to the market goods of higher value than those provided in the past, but the increased value does not necessarily decrease the amount you pay.

The fecklessness of the conservatives was underscored by their reaction when the president finally revealed the details of his plan in September 1993. Two days after the announcement, Newt Gingrich appeared with Clinton lackey George Stephanopoulos on the Charlie Rose show on PBS. Gingrich was so uncritical of the president's program that Rose had difficulty distinguishing Gingrich's views from Stephanopoulos'. By show's end, Rose declared their debate a "lovefest."

Happily, not all conservatives were so spineless or unintelligent. If most of the conservative leadership resigned itself to the scheme, hoping only to soften its impact, much of the conservative rank-and-file remained dubious. Their hostility to the plan was strengthened by the herculean efforts of bombastic radio personality Rush Limbaugh, who never wavered in his opposition to the Clinton plan.

As time wore on and the horrible details of the Clinton plan became manifest, public opinion turned against it. Perhaps the most significant single event in the battle was the publication of Elizabeth McCaughey's analysis of the plan in *The New Republic* (February 7, 1994). McCaughey had an advantage over almost all the proponents and the critics of the bill alike: she actually read it in its entirety. Her piece was simply devastating — all the more so because it was published in an establishment journal that had supported Clinton.

Out of the Crisis

President Clinton was surely right when he said, "This health care system of ours is badly broken, and it is time to fix it." But any solution is going to have to come from outside the borders of the debate that were established by conservatives, left-liberals, and vested interests. It requires an examination of the cause of the health care crisis, and an exploration of how we got into the mess we're in.

The crisis in medical care is a matter of very basic economics. Normally, people's demand for goods and services is elastic and limited. When the price of a good goes up, people buy less of it. I love hamburgers. At current restaurant prices of $2 to $6, I average a couple of burgers each week. But if the price rose to $20, I would eat fewer, and if it went to $100, I would eliminate them from my diet entirely. My demand for burgers is price-sensitive, "elastic."

In America today, demand for health care is both inelastic and virtually unlimited. That is to say, people want the absolute best health care and could not care less about the cost, since in most cases it is paid for by their government or employer. When demand for any economic good is inelastic and unlimited, the price must shoot upward.

Suppose for a moment that every one of us could have all the hamburgers we wanted, made from the finest ingredients, prepared by the best-trained chefs, and that all these burgers were paid for by someone else. What would happen to the price of burgers?

Would the price of burgers fall, because people wanted more of them? If a burger cost you nothing, would you go to a cut-rate restaurant? Would you seek burgers made from cheap ingredients?

Would the costs of the burger industry fall? Would it become more efficient? Or would costs rise as more and more research went into making better burgers, as finer and finer cuts of beef were ground into burger patties?

Now suppose that burger chefs were allowed to restrict the number of people allowed to enter the burger profession. What would happen to the salaries demanded by burger chefs? What effect would this have on the price of burgers?

This is precisely what has happened with medical care. Most Americans are entitled, by virtue of medical insurance provided by their employer or by welfare payments provided by their government, to whatever medical care they want or need, no matter what the expense. The cost of medical care has skyrocketed in the same way the cost of burgers would skyrocket if we were all allowed whatever burgers we want without the obligation of paying for them. Add to this the effects of medical licensing, with its consequent cartelization, and ever-higher costs are assured.

Government guarantees of payment for certain heroic medical procedures have further accelerated the rising cost of medical care. At present, for example, certain medical procedures are routinely performed to extend the life of an elderly patient by only a few months at a cost to taxpayers of hundreds of thousands of dollars. If government did not guarantee these payments, the incidence of these heroic procedures would be far less frequent. Most families would simply not be able to afford them, and many of those who could would decide against doing so. If briefly extending the life of an elderly parent means selling one's home and denying one's children an education, most Americans would reluctantly decide not to do so. Such procedures would be performed mostly on the very wealthy or on people who have chosen to forgo the purchase of other goods for the security of insurance that covers such treatment.

This is at least slightly offensive to most people's egalitarian impulses. But who is to say that this method of rationing heroic medical care is better than outlawing heroic procedures altogether, the method typically used where medical care is socialized?

The root of the problem is that most Americans believe that all of us have a *right* to the best health care, no matter what the cost. Implicitly or explicitly, almost all Americans are reluctant to deny a person medical care — leave a person to suffer or die — because he cannot afford to pay a physician or a hospital for their services.

The Root of the Problem

So long as Americans have a broad consensus in favor of guaranteeing every American unlimited care regardless of cost, the price of health will rise sharply. Health care is excellent for those who can afford it — for the rich, for employees of firms that provide extensive medical benefits, and for those elderly, poor, and government-employed Americans whose medical expenses are paid from Uncle Sam's "infinitely deep" pockets. These groups comprise about 75% of all Americans. The remainder — mostly the self-employed, people between jobs, and those who work for smaller businesses that don't provide insurance — are increasingly being priced out of the market.

These people are the worst victims of the present system. To keep its costs from skyrocketing totally out of control, the government has mandated spending limits on certain procedures — limits that are often below costs. Large employer-provided insurance also often negotiates maximum payments for services, though usually at a level than can cover costs. This leaves only one group of people to pay for the physician's or hospital's losses on Medicare and Medicaid patients — those without insurance.

Medical care comprises about 15% of the American economy. Is it a wise policy to turn such a huge industry over to management by a single presidentially-appointed board? Would such a board be able to provide flexibility or entrepreneurship? Would it have the foresight to finance useful research and to manage that research efficiently? What are the chances that a government takeover would result in much higher costs, rather than the savings promised by the Clintons? (When Medicare was proposed in 1965, President Lyndon Johnson estimated that in 1990, it would cost a total of $8 billion. The actual cost in 1990 was $98 billion — more than twelve times LBJ's projection.)

The root of the problem of ever-escalating medical costs is government subsidy of medical care — not just for the poor and elderly, but for ordinary citizens (through tax incentives given large employers). So long as those subsidies are in place and no effective limits are placed on them, demand will continue to grow and costs will continue to escalate. The problem of red tape is caused by feeble government attempts to control costs, by placing limits on procedures covered and requiring hospitals and physicians to report their services in detail.

The solution to these problems is not to redouble government subsidy and control. The solution is to radically reduce government subsidy and control.

Solving the health care crisis is simple. But it will not be easy. Americans must come to understand that medical care ought to be subject to the same considerations as any other economic good. Medical care is often as vital as food — but no more vital. The arguments against socializing medicine are precisely the same as those against socializing food, clothing, or shelter. We must understand that sometimes, some people will not be able to afford medical care that they need. We must understand that buying better medical care means buying less of some other goods — less travel, or less entertainment, or less extravagant food or housing. Medical care must become like any other commodity, subject to the same individual evaluations, the same forces of supply and demand, if the good is to be made efficiently available.

The root of the idea that medical care is fundamentally different from other economic goods lies in the humanitarian impulse that every human being ought to get medical care, whether he can afford it or not. This natural impulse has never been consistently applied by those who advocate it. While it is plausible to provide medical care to the indigent of one's community, or perhaps even to all the indigent in the entire country, it is manifest that neither the American taxpayer nor all the taxpayers in the world can foot the bill for the world's four billion poor.

Living Without Miracles

Until recently, the cost of providing medical care to the indigent has been low enough that it seemed plausible to pay the bill from voluntary charity or from relatively modest increases in taxes. In the early years of this century, medicine consisted mostly of sending lovable ol' Doc Spencer over into the poor section of town to dispense a few pills. But as science progressed, medical technology grew more effective, more complicated, and more expensive.

Yet the notion of a universal right to medical care was saved by the institutionalization of charity. When government and large employers took over responsibility for paying for medical care, the feedback provided by consumer demand was no longer looped back to allocate assets and control costs. The myth of a right to universal medical care was given new life, but with medical care providers no longer constrained by the consumers' ability and willingness to pay, costs skyrocketed, threatening to bankrupt the nation.

The outlook is not good. If the conservatives have their way, and nothing is done, prices will continue to spiral out of control. If the left-liberals have their way, the country will be saddled with a Soviet-style system, in which medical care will be rationed by bureaucrats and committees, in which costs will rise while quality deteriorates.

In the wake of the defeat of the Clinton proposal, Congress has passed a compromise measure with support from both Republicans and Democrats. The Kennedy-Kassebaum bill incorporates some of the worst features of the Clintons' plan.

It guarantees universal eligibility for health insurance. This means that insurance companies must offer insurance to individuals already diagnosed with expensive-to-treat diseases on the same basis as healthy individuals. As Sheldon Richman has observed, this is like requiring insurers to sell life insurance to people who are already dead.

This requirement is bound to increase premiums for individuals who are not already sick. Faced with rising insurance costs, many such individuals, especially those who are young and healthy, will drop their insurance. Removing the young and healthy from the pool of those insured will then increase costs — and thus premiums — further still.

The bill guarantees that mental health will be treated on an equal basis as physical health, thereby guaranteeing psychological counseling and therapy free of any cost to the user. Inevitably, this will drive up the demand for such counseling, adding further to the skyrocketing cost of insurance.

In short, the ultimate effect of the bill will be to drive insurance rates sharply upward, and thus to increase pressure for a total government takeover.

These measures enjoyed widespread support among Republicans in the House and *unanimous* support among Republicans in the Senate. This strongly suggests that the GOP's belated criticism of the Clinton bill represented political opportunism at its worst, attacking a measure as a means of attacking a man, rather than any real understanding of the problems state intervention has caused within the U.S. medical system.

There are two major differences between the House and

Senate versions, which is before a joint committee for final resolution as I write these words. The House version copies more or less intact provisions from the Clintons' bill that provide a raft of bizarre penalties for physicians who make even trivial mistakes in dealing with insurance companies. Among its penalties:

> . . . five years in prison for making a misstatement to your health plan (say you "forgot" to mention a pre-existing condition); ten years in prison for intentionally "misapplying" any assets of the plan (say to a "medically unnecessary" service that nonetheless relieves your symptoms); one year in prison if the "misapplied" amount is less than $100; five years in prison for failing to turn over a patient's records (say to a prosecutor who wants to accuse him of making a misstatement to the plan); life in prison if a plan is "defrauded" in connection with the care of a patient who dies.
>
> And that's not all. The bill also calls for fines of $10,000 for each instance of "incorrect" coding, even an honest mistake, on insurance claims (there are thousands of codes and no consistent interpretation); fines and/or prison for those who "transfer items or services for free or for other than fair market value" (i.e., who provide unauthorized charity); automatic seizure of all property paid for with the gross proceeds of any "federal health care offense" (and all offenses related to any health insurance plan, public or private, will be federal offenses).
>
> The message sent by the Kassebaum-Kennedy bill is loud and clear: Any doctor who practices fee-for-service medicine has to put it all on the line — his house, his car, his office, his bank accounts, and most of all, his liberty. If he "fails to comply with a statutory obligation" to provide only "medically necessary" services, correctly coded, be can be reduced to lifelong poverty and imprisoned besides. The law enforcement machinery will be vastly augmented to meet the challenge. There will be rewards to informants, and prosecutors get to keep the fines and seized property. If the enforcers need evidence, they can seize anybody's medical records anytime. ("Health Bill Would Shackle Doctors," by Jane M. Orient, M.D., *The Wall Street Journal* , May 30, 1996. Dr. Orient is the executive director of the Association of American Physicians and Surgeons.)

The version of the bill passed by the Senate, meanwhile, specifies that physician errors are subject to such horrible penalties only if they are "knowing and willful."

The House version also authorizes Medical Savings Accounts. If this measure were enacted into law, an individual could deposit a portion of his or her income into a savings account, from which he or she could pay ordinary medical bills and purchase catastrophic insurance coverage. Deposits made into the MSA would be tax-deductible in the same way that employer-paid insurance premiums are. A person would be able eventually to convert his MSA to personal use, so he would have an incentive to spend his money prudently.

It is this sensible reform that threatens the final passage of the measure. Clinton has indicated he will veto any bill that includes any provision for Medical Savings Accounts, but the House seems adamant about keeping the provision

The final outcome is a lose-lose situation, unless the measure is allowed to die completely. If the president prevails, we get all the provisions that will make the problem of soaring medical costs worse, without the mitigating influence of Medical Savings Accounts. If the House GOP prevails, we get all the soaring costs of the original measure, mitigated somewhat by the MSAs. And maybe the final measure will include the Orwellian provisions punishing physicians who do not work for HMOs for the tiniest clerical error. (There is a modest chance that the stalemate will not be resolved, and that no measure at all will be enacted. We should have such luck!)

A sensible system — one in which costs are controlled by market forces and progress is financed by consumer demand — can be purchased only at the cost of the realization that miracles are not within the power of government, that the laws of economics apply to *all* consumer goods, even medical care, and that unlimited health care cannot ever be the birthright of all Americans.

Whether Americans will be willing to pay that price remains to be seen.

Behind the Task-Force Veil

by Richard D. Fisher

"If the forces arrayed against reform want a real battle in which their self-interest is exposed and their real agenda is made public, they will get it."

—*Hillary Rodham Clinton, November 9, 1993*

We all remember the President's Task Force on Health Care Reform, a collection of "experts" assembled by Ira Magaziner in January 1993 to develop a plan to reform America's medical care system. In February 1993, the Association of American Physicians and Surgeons filed suit under the Federal Advisory Committee Act (FACA) to force the Clinton administration to reveal the task force's composition. In November, the administration was ordered to comply. The documents thus made public suggest a very different picture of the task force than the White House has presented.

The task force consisted of 15 cluster groups, 43 working groups, and four subgroups. The leaders of over half of these, as well as many of the participants, were representatives of private managed-care interests with much to gain should the Clinton health plan be enacted. Among the special interests represented were United Health Care Corporation, Chicago Health Maintenance Organization, Aetna, Travelers, Liberty Mutual Insurance, Wausau Insurance Company, National Capital Preferred Providers Organization, Harvard Community Health Plan, Kaiser Permanente, U.S. Health Care, EDS Health Care, PCS Health Systems, First Health, Blue Cross/Blue Shield, and Alliant Health Systems.

Remember the Health Security Card that Bill Clinton brandished so proudly on national television? One corporation represented on the task force was MCI Communications — the likely primary vendor for the 250 million cards that Clinton's plan would require. Potential contractors for other parts of the Clinton plan were also amply represented, including the Rand Corporation, Alpha Center, Telesis, Cooper & Lybrand, Price Waterhouse, and the Principal Financial Group.

FACA was not the only law the task force tried to circumvent. All executive personnel, including special government employees, were required by the Ethics in Government Act to file conflict-of-interest forms. But only 35 of these special government employees and consultants did so. Of those, many were submitted months late. Almost all were filled out in the handwriting of someone other than the filer, some in two different handwritings, and some with dates typed over correction fluid.

It is plain that Robert Berenson, president of National Capital Preferred Provider Organization; Lois Quam, vice president of United Health Care Organization; and David Eddy, advisor to Kaiser Permanente, had conflicts of interest in helping formulate federal health-care policy. Yet these officials and executives of major managed-care concerns played significant task-force roles without obtaining waivers for conflicts of interest, despite the requirements of law. Indeed, *not one* consultant obtained the required waiver.

A Shaky Foundation

Few organizations have put as much money and work into the campaign for government-run medicine as the Robert Wood Johnson Foundation. With over $90 million in demonstration grants, leveraged with the requirement for matching funds from taxpayers, the RWJF has seduced eleven state governments into implementing managed-care plans.

The RWJF — along with the Henry J. Kaiser Family Foundation and the Urban Institute — tried to use the task force to do the same thing on a national level. They developed the format for the task force structure and asked their own people and other grant recipients to help put together the Clinton plan. Fellows salaried by the foundation posed as full-time staffers for Senators Rockefeller, Bumpers, Bradley, Kennedy, and Wofford to obviate FACA requirements. They actively participated in many of the task force's cluster groups and subgroups. In addition, Assistant HHS Secretary Judith Feder was both a senior investigator for the RWJF and a full-time government employee while working for the task force.

At the same time, the foundation gave substantial grants to George Washington University to sponsor so-called "public forums" on health care reform across the country. Similar programs were funded by the Kaiser Foundation with the League of Women Voters Education Fund. Proffered as free and open forums for the discussion of medical care reform issues, these forums were in fact little more than community outreach propaganda mills for Clinton's health plan. And NBC News accepted $2.5 million from the RWJF to produce a two-hour special on health care. The propaganda war moves on.

Getting Past the Lies

Rather than admit to the prominent participation of special interests in formulating its health-care proposals, the White House chose the path of secrecy and closed doors. In doing so, it trampled on the law. The bill itself would have trampled on a lot more.

Ira Magaziner's task force was a sham — and so was its product, the Health Care Security Act. It was no surprise that the act featured a large and government-subsidized role for managed care. Nor was it surprising that it would have done little to improve the American medical care system, and a lot to make it worse.

The Magaziner task force is but one more chapter in a sad but familiar story, one in which private special interests and tax-exempt foundations insinuate themselves into the legislative and executive branches of government to create policies that benefit themselves and those they seek to promote. The ultimate victim, again, is the American public.

Old-Growth Pork
by Randal O'Toole

Most observers at the President's Conference on Northwest Forests, sensitized to the polarization between the timber industry and environmentalists, focused on whether the spotted owls or loggers were winning, or which were getting in the most "hits." Perhaps because I just got back from Washington, D.C., my focus was a little different.

In downtown Washington, shabbily dressed panhandlers occupy nearly every street corner, seeking donations from the lobbyists, financiers, and diplomats on their way to work or lunch. Some of the panhandlers sing, some tell stories ("I need another quarter for bus fare"), some just hold out paper cups. Many people are disgusted by the beggars, but the panhandlers apparently earn enough to keep going or there wouldn't be so many of them.

A much more respectable, yet far more destructive, form of panhandling takes place over at the Capitol. Well-dressed lobbyists line up before congressional committees to sing their songs and tell their stories about why the taxpayer should pay for their pet projects. I was far more disgusted by them than by the beggars outside, though I suspect I am eccentric in this respect.

Nearly everyone appearing before the Interior Subcommittee hearings of the House Appropriations Committee, whose hearings I attended the week before the forest conference, asked for more money for some park, forest, or range project. The testimony became very predictable: a park association asks for money for their park, a hardwood manufacturer association asks for more money for hardwood research, an environmental group asks for more money for buying land.

A few people asked that the committee spend less on one item and more on another. I was the only one who wanted an overall reduction in spending. The committee just laughed at the idea.

So as the forest conference approached, I had pork on my mind. Just before the conference, I wrote a policy paper predicting that at least four pork programs — thinnings, ecosystem restoration, increasing payments to counties, and banning log exports — would be proposed. They would cost taxpayers hundreds of millions of dollars, I suggested, while doing little good for the environment.

All of these and more were proposed at the conference. It turns out I had underestimated the creativity which people would use to design pork barrel projects. Many people talked about "incentives." Not market incentives, but tax and subsidy incentives.

Here are a few examples:

- John Gordon, member of the "Gang of Four,"* wanted money for habitat restoration and more money for research. (Ask a researcher what ought to be done and the answer will always include more research.)

- Jim Sedell, hydrologist and honorary Gang of Four member, suggested we begin watershed planning. (We wasted billions on forest planning, but drawing the planning units along watershed boundaries will magically fix the problems. Sorry. Been there. Done that. Doesn't work. The Forest Service did watershed planning in the 1970s and it was as inept as anything a Soviet planner ever tried.)

- Ecologist Jerry Franklin suggested that we train and hire rural people to do forest monitoring. (*What happens to the workers when we run out of money for such monitoring?* I

---

* The Scientific Panel on Late-Succession Ecosystems, four eminent scientists charged by Congress with developing plans for management of Northwest old-growth forests. They developed 32 different management options, all consonant with their conclusion that all remaining old-growth forest needs to be preserved to assure a high degree of viability for old-growth species.

asked Jerry. "We won't ever run out," he said, "the government can just print more." Remember when they said we would never run out of old-growth timber?)

- Bob Lee, a forest sociologist, wanted to do "community-based planning." (See above. One problem with planning is that we don't trust anyone to do it — not planners, not economists, not communities, not governments, not corporations. If no one can be trusted to do something, why do we keep wanting to do it?)

- Meca Wawona, an ecosystem restorationist from the California Redwoods, wanted to spend billions on restoration, to do for the Northwest what the Redwood Park bill did for northern California. (But just what is restoration? I am sure that, to some, it includes road construction, clear-cutting, dams, and all kinds of other activities that Meca does not want. No matter how carefully designed, a pork barrel is a pork barrel is a pork barrel.)

- Bob Doppelt, of the Pacific Rivers Council, put some numbers on his proposal: $750 million for fish habitat restoration. (I wonder if Bob knew that a fish biologist in Douglas County told Bruce Babbitt that "what the fish here need most is three more dams." I am sure that was music to the ears of the former Arizona governor and longtime supporter of the Central Arizona Project.)

- Roslyn Heffner, a vocational counsellor, suggested tax breaks or reduced workmen's compensation for companies that hire unemployed loggers (making everyone else pay their share).

- Chad Oliver of the University of Washington hinted at tax breaks for timber companies practicing New Forestry (old subsidies for new forestry?).

- Not to be outdone, Brian Greber of Oregon State

University, promoted tax breaks for companies engaged in "growth" industries such as composites. (If the industry is doing so well, why does it need our money?)

Not everyone wanted pork. When University of Oregon economist Ed Whitelaw was asked about log exports, he acted embarrassed that he didn't have any pork to offer; he just muttered something about leveling the playing field with Japan, which has higher tariffs on imports of processed lumber than on raw logs.

If the environmentalists seemed more subdued than the rest of the presenters, it was partly because most of them weren't offering the president any juicy bits of pork that he could hand out the Northwest. Andy Kerr briefly mentioned fixing the Forest Service's incentives, but also wanted to ban log exports. Felice Pace went so far as to urge that the market should be left alone.

To paraphrase Al Gore (who noted that "it probably isn't a coincidence that all of the senators opposing the president's pork barrel — I mean, economic recovery package — are Republicans"), it probably isn't a coincidence that most of the invited speakers advocated some sort of pork. For the first time since at least 1969, we have a president who truly believes that pork barrel is good for the economy, that government can solve problems, and that the democratic process counts for more than economic substance.

But the forest conference wasn't really about pork barrel, any more than it was about spotted owls. The conference was about process.

What other president would drag his vice president, four cabinet secretaries, and assorted other top officials all the way across the country to hold a town meeting discussing essentially a local problem? Franklin Roosevelt, maybe? Probably someone well before him.

One reason this seems so unimaginable today is that the federal government is so much bigger than it was a few decades ago. When Franklin Roosevelt took office, the entire federal budget was not much more than the Forest Service alone spends today. Roosevelt and presidents before him could take the time to deal with local or peripheral problems. Not today. The $3.5 billion-per-year Forest Service budget is barely a gnat's eyelash on the brow of the federal giant.

But Clinton took the time. He listened, he asked sensible (if pre-programmed) questions, and he hardly ever appeared bored. The questions that Gore and the cabinet secretaries asked appeared to be mostly off-the-cuff, and dialog was minimized more by the nervousness of the presenters than by the loftiness of the president and his team.

So Clinton was doing far more than just keeping a campaign promise. He was sending a signal about his style of presidency and his idea about what government can and should do.

And after the conference, he produced his own Northwest forest plan — one about as bad as it could be without actually detonating nuclear devices. The president seems to believe that old standby that if you make everyone mad, you must be doing something right. So his plan puts thousands of people out of work, shuts down many sawmills, and still leaves a significant chance that the spotted owl and many other species will go extinct.

The plan's centerpiece provides token benefits to the timber industry by allowing salvage logging in old-growth reserves, despite most ecologists' recommendations against such logging. This logging does little to mitigate old-growth protection's impact on the northwest timber industry, but greatly increases the risk that more species will be listed as threatened or endangered. Perhaps this is what Clinton means by a "balanced approach."

But the real story is that the plan proposes to spend billions of dollars on programs whose benefits are negligible, proving once again that what the president really believes in is pork. In most cases, the proposals amount to robbing Peter to pay Paul. For example, a proposal to create secondary wood-manufacturing jobs, if enacted, will put people in other parts of the country out of work as their factories close to move to the Northwest.

Clinton would also limit the sale of timber from some forests to mills that will process the wood in specified communities. This won't save a single job — it just means that the mills that will survive will be those with political pull rather than those able to process the wood most efficiently. It will also cost taxpayers plenty, since limited competition will shrink the bid prices for timber.

Clinton's experts estimate that the old-growth reserves will cost 6,000 direct jobs, and he proposes to spend $1.2 billion to mitigate those losses. That's $200,000 per job — but most of the money will be spent by federal, state, and local bureaucracies before the workers see any benefits. No wonder the state governors support the plan.

The president also promises to subject the Northwest to another round of forest planning. The last round cost over a billion dollars and failed to resolve a single issue. This one will be more expensive still because the agencies will rely on high-tech computer databases that draw pretty maps. The maps will be completely wrong, because no one will actually bother to collect any data from the forest.

The plan includes some rhetoric about increasing timber supplies. Private landowners with spotted owls may be allowed to cut a little more timber if they promise not to export the logs. The federal government will provide more subsidies to timber programs on Indian reservations. But these actions will have little effect on timber prices.

The good news is that wood prices aren't likely to get any higher because most of the effects of reduced timber sales have already been felt by the market. Northwest loggers will be allowed to cut more timber than they've been cutting in the past few years. Of course, Clinton first has to convince Judge Dwyer to lift the legal injunctions on timber sales, and his staff is busy twisting the arms of environmental groups to get them to agree to this.

How did the president come up with such a stinker? After his Conference on Northwest Forests, he locked up a few hundred agency bureaucrats in a room and told them to write a plan. No one should be surprised that its prime beneficiaries are not the sawmills or the environmentalists but the bureaucrats who wrote it.

For example, most of the writers were scientists. So of course their plan calls for dedicating tens of millions of dollars to new research. It even sets aside over two million acres of forest for "ecological experimentation."

When all the costs of planning and lost timber receipts are added to the $1.2 billion "jobs" package, the plan will cost tax-payers "only" about $3 to $4 billion over the next five years. The really bad news is that the president considers this process a model for solving all environmental problems.

This means that governors of states whose industries are threatened by environmental lawsuits can look forward to Clinton dropping a few billion dollars on them to "solve" the problem without actually saving either the environment or the industries. Just hope no one asks where the money is coming from.

Instead of porking out, Clinton *could* have used the forest conference as an opportunity for "reinventing government" along the lines of the book of that name. Like most public land controversies, the old-growth issue is rooted in the fact that the Forest Service and related agencies are top-heavy bureaucracies that reward managers with bigger budgets when they lose money.

The solution is to change the system of rewards that managers face. This means, first, removing the incentive to lose money by funding managers out of their net income, not out of tax dollars. Second, promoting true multiple-use management by allowing agencies to charge fair market value for all resources, including recreation. Third, allowing groups who object to timber sales to bid on such sales and, if they win, *not* cut them down. Wilderness and certain other user fees could provide seed money for such "conservation easements."

In short, take forest issues out of the political arena and into the marketplace, where they can be resolved without polarization. Clinton missed this possibility when he relied on the agencies themselves, which would naturally resist any proposal to shrink their budgets, to write his plan for him. The forest plan's real winners are neither environmentalists nor loggers but bureaucrats and pork-eaters. The real losers are not spotted owls or consumers but the taxpayers who will have to pay for it all.

Trading Away Free Trade
by Fred L. Smith, Jr.

The General Agreement on Tariffs and Trade has lowered the world's tariff barriers fairly well. Its proponents — including the Cato Institute and other libertarian groups — argue that the latest modification to GATT, the World Trade Organization, will advance free trade even further. So does the Clinton administration, which negotiated the final agreement, and so do most large businesses. It is opposed by a handful of populists like Ralph Nader and Pat Buchanan, with environmental and labor groups withholding support until further "protections" are added.

The WTO builds on GATT's base, adding trade in services and intellectual property to the trade in goods already covered by GATT. It is being sold as a global equivalent of the interstate commerce clause of the U.S. Constitution, as a guarantee of the right to buy and sell goods throughout the world. But it may prove instead to be more like the Interstate Commerce Commission — a tool for the cartelization of economic activity, the exploitation of consumers, and the suppression of economic liberty.

Revamping GATT

Free trade needn't involve foreign entanglements. It requires only that nations remove their own barriers to international exchange. But protectionism is a powerful force, and few legislators are eager to confront special interests out to escape foreign competition. So they pander to producers whose goods are blocked from other countries' markets. Usually, they try to open those markets with "retaliation": "if you don't open your borders to my goods, I'll block your goods from my markets." This strategy rarely works even on its own terms; as Jim Powell has pointed out, "it is hard to find a single significant case in which trade retaliation or retaliatory threats have forced open a foreign market" ("Why Trade Retaliation Closes Markets and Impoverishes People," *Cato Policy Analysis* #143).

GATT also relies on trade retaliation. Nations bring disputes before GATT, and a panel is convened to judge the merits of the charges. If a country is found guilty of blocking trade, the offended nation is entitled to impose penalties against the offender's imports. Despite its authorization of this dubious practice, GATT seems to have worked fairly well: tariffs have been gradually reduced and world trade has increased. It is important to remember, though, that the system was never intended to promote free trade *per se*. Lower tariffs and increased trade may have occurred despite GATT as much as because of it.

At the same time, lower tariffs have increased the importance of other forms of protectionism. These new restraints are inherently more difficult to resolve — or detect. Unmodified cars are difficult to sell in England or Japan, where people drive on the left side of the road. Is this a trade barrier? Aggressive exporters convinced of the superiority of their products and selling abilities are too quick to see non-tariff barriers where brand loyalty, price or quality differences, lack of repair facilities, or already well-established trading patterns are to blame for their problems. To hear some firms tell it, *any* lack of sales is a result of foreign protectionism.

Will the WTO erase real impediments to free trade, or will it pander to fears of pantomime protectionism? You have to wonder.

For one thing, by widening the range of products covered by GATT, the WTO widens the scope of cross-retaliation against products not involved in the original dispute. Thus, the WTO sharpens the sting of trade sanctions by allowing governments to punish each other in ways that cause the most pain, dragging unrelated businesses into a trade dispute: an American software firm, for example, might be punished in retaliation for an American agricultural firm selling rice too cheaply in Japan.

Clinton's negotiators, not known for their staunch free trade principles, incorporated some troublesome aspects of U.S. anti-dumping and countervailing duties laws into the GATT agreement, legitimizing the protectionist rules of the U.S. International Trade Commission and the Department of Commerce. European nations, in turn, insisted on explicitly defining their industrial-policy subsidies as acceptable trading practices. The Clintonites accepted these changes, which allow them to expand the domestic subsidies *they* wish to pursue. Combined with the European demand to allow export rebates for energy taxes, GATT's subsidy provisions could encourage European-style industrial policy in the U.S. and other nations.

Because the Uruguay Round of international tariff-reduction negotiations must be ratified as a trade agreement, the WTO will enjoy an enhanced status as its global enforcement arm. The voting rules of this bureaucracy are different from those of the old GATT, where decisions were made by consensus and voting procedures were rarely invoked. Like the United Nations General Assembly, every nation, regardless of size, will have an equal vote in the WTO. Larger nations will receive no Security Council-style veto, nor will they benefit from weighted voting, as in the World Bank and the International Monetary Fund. Moreover, unlike the old GATT, the WTO envisions incremental, one-at-a-time modifications in trade rules, each voted on separately. GATT rounds, by contrast, were package deals — complex sets of negotiated tariff reductions across a wide array of goods traded by many nations.

The United States found it much easier to close unnecessary military bases with a GATT-style package deal than with the WTO's incremental approach. Will similar incentive problems hamper efforts to reduce trade barriers?

Moreover, the WTO rules encourage "public participation,"

ensuring a change in the forces influencing future trade disputes. Mickey Kantor's claims that these rules will make it easier for citizens' interests to be represented are not to be believed. In the U.S., "public participation" has become a code phrase for granting extraordinary powers to narrow pressure groups. The all-too-likely beneficiaries of the public-participation provisions will be the "progressive" activist groups that have done so much to politicize the U.S. economy.

One danger inherent in an unweighted, veto-free voting system is that such groups could work with foreign protectionists to advance the ideologues' domestic agendas. For example, a German firm might argue that America's lower rates of recycling or higher rates of energy consumption are "non-sustainable," and thus constitute an unfair trading practice. The EC has already effectively excluded Spanish beer from German markets by requiring that all beer be sold in reusable bottles.

Deceptive Greenspeak

The Clinton Administration, supported by France and other nations, has pushed for a commission to consider how the WTO system should be modified to advance "fair," "sustainable," and "socially just" trade. The dominant multinational corporations, non-governmental organizations (NGOs), environmental activist groups, and government elites seem in general agreement that a more tightly managed world trading system is preferable to a free one. In this context, one has to wonder whether the WTO will advance or retard economic liberty.

The WTO's preamble already incorporates hortatory requirements that trade be compatible with government-defined environmental goals and that it encourage "sustainable development." America's experience with environmental laws provide good reasons to take such rhetoric seriously. The 1972 Clean Water Act gives the federal government regulatory authority over the navigable waters of the United States. Who could have dreamt that "navigable waters" would one day be inter-preted so broadly as to allow the EPA and Army Corps of Engineers to impose land use controls on hundreds of millions of acres of private property under the guise of protecting "wetlands"?

Radical reinterpretations of such clear language have charac-terized most domestic environmental statutes — the Endangered Species Act, various hazardous waste laws, recycling mandates, etc. Why should we believe that free marketeers will be any bet-ter at stopping encroachments on "clear language" in the future than they have been in the past?

Our past experience with multinational agreements is cause for pessimism. When George Bush signed the Global Climate Convention in Rio, he assured us that it would be non-binding. Now the Clinton-Gore administration has informed us that it *is* binding, committing the U.S. to reducing carbon dioxide emis-sions to 1990 levels by the year 2000. This administration has also suggested that the treaty may be used to raise fuel economy standards, extending a deadly regulation that already causes thousands of highway fatalities each year. George Bush also signed Agenda 21, the Earth Summit's blueprint for "sustainable development" policies, including new restrictions on global commerce rationalized on environmental grounds. The U.N. Development Programme proposes a global trade levy as an ini-tial means to that end.

The WTO's preamble, along with Keynesian goals of "effec-tive demand" and "full employment," affirms the need for a greening of trade:

- It asserts the importance of "allowing for the optimal use of the world's resources in accordance with the objective of sustainable development, seeking both to protect and preserve the environment and enhance the means for doing so. . . ."

- WTO nations are committed to "harmonize" their technical regulations and sanitary standards. Provision is made for nations to adopt measures different from international standards, but only if they are more stringent. Downward harmonization is officially discouraged, though not prohibited — yet.

- The dispute settlement understanding allows nations and arbitration panels to seek scientific and technical advice from any individual or organization. NGOs will enjoy more "public participation" rights under these procedures.

- The Clinton administration fought to establish a WTO Committee on Trade and the Environment at the insistence of Sen. Max Baucus (D-Mont.) and other congressional environmentalists. It will develop modifications to WTO policies in order to support "sustainable development," including economic instruments, pollution charges and environmental taxes, compulsory recycling, regulation of processes and production methods, packaging and labelling requirements, and "public participation" rights. It may review any trade-related issue, including carbon taxes, levies on fossil fuels, and transportation restrictions.

- Thanks to French and American pressure, a general committee will address how the WTO can ensure "basic rights" for workers — i.e., labor laws that produce unemployment.

Some analysts assert that such managed trade policies merely represent a desirable extension of the Hayekian rule of law. That is nonsense. Hayek saw no virtue in harmonization or standardization for its own sake. He reminded us that legislation works best where customs, values, and language are already shared. This world is not such a place. Attempting to impose a "rule of law" on the international trading system via the WTO, or any other centralized organization, will be a complex and most likely ill-fated enterprise. Uniform rules that evolve through voluntary arrangements are beneficial; those imposed by some exogenous authority are not.

The New World Trading Order

The WTO's political centralization could come at the expense of our decentralized federal-state-local relationships. Writing in *Commentary*, Jeremy Rabkin effectively describes what is at stake:

> Sovereignty is not a matter of legal formalities .. . . [The] erosion of sovereignty entails a blurring of the lines of accountability. . . . [T]he internationalization of our domestic policy disputes adds one more — and potentially much larger and more intricate — layer of technical confusion between public preferences and the excuses of politicians not to respond to them. It makes government that much more obscure, remote, and inaccessible to ordinary citizens.

Consider our disastrous experiences with other global bureaucracies. GATT worked fairly well under its consensus rules, but it is an exception. More common is the phenomenal mischief-making of the World Bank and IMF, which have repeatedly destroyed economies, bailed out state socialism, and — despite their newfound environmentalist rhetoric — wreaked enormous ecological damage. Recent internal audits of the World Bank revealed a 37.5% failure rate on its lending projects. Few IMF loan recipients have become economically self-sufficient, and IMF conditionality arrangements have led to increased taxation, "balanced" trade policies, and other destructive statist programs.

Institutions are shaped by the incentives they create. GATT's focus on reducing tariffs encouraged a pro-trade bureaucracy. By contrast, the U.S. International Trade Commission, the Commerce Department, and the U.S. Trade Representative are charged with ensuring "fair" trade; for that reason, they have never been proponents of free trade, even under the nominally anti-protectionist Reagan administration

At the WTO, U.S. economic interests are all too likely to promote a quota approach to trade policy, to find "unfairness" in any lack of market penetration, to see the use of a language other than English as a non-tariff barrier. And U.S. ideological interests are all too likely to use the WTO to promote a "social trade" agenda.

Exploiting the Third World

Some WTO proponents have seen virtue in the power the one-nation-one-vote system gives to smaller nations, arguing that the Third World has a strong stake in free trade and will counterbalance the regulatory demands of the U.S., Europe, and Japan. But experience with existing environmental treaties suggests they are wrong.

The International Whaling Commission was intended to ensure sustainable harvesting of whales, but has been transformed into an anti-development, pro-animal-rights statute. Even Norway's Prime Minister Gro Harlem Brundtland, the Joan of Arc of the Earth Summit, cannot control this process; recently, she charged the Clinton-Gore administration with caring more about whales than about people. Yet few of the world's nations care enough to oppose the movement to ban whaling — and those that do were outvoted by the NGO-influenced majority of nations.

Much of the Third World supported the Basel Convention, an agreement based on the premise that trade in hazardous waste services should be avoided wherever possible. Likewise, developing countries signed on to the Convention on Trade in Endangered Species (CITES), pushed by European and American environmental establishment groups seeking publicity and funding. The effect of CITES is to punish nations with sound conservation programs. A handful of African nations are beginning to have second thoughts about CITES, but so far too few to yet have an impact.

These experiences illustrate that developing nations are an ineffective force for free trade. Worse, they demonstrate that Third World elites have no compunction against betraying their own people for personal gain. Foreign aid cannot compensate the world for the damage done by protectionism and regulation, but it can buy a lot of environmentalist Uncle Toms ready to sell their fellow citizens down the river. Will the Third World be crucified on a cross of green?

Global Cartels

The late nineteenth century was the era of robber-baron capitalism and rapid economic growth. For the first time, many firms were operating at a national level. The interstate commerce clause prevented Balkanization, while the lack of any federal political entity able to protect a specific firm, to "regulate" commerce, made cartelization impossible. Competition was inevitable and the nation prospered.

Neither business nor politicians nor the "public interest" community were happy about this. In the late nineteenth century, economic interests (railroads out to suppress competition) and ideological interests (anti-market Progressives) pushed for a federal body able to restrain competition. Together, this Baptist-Bootlegger coalition succeeded in creating the Interstate Commerce Commission, which suppressed transportation competition for almost 100 years under the guise of harmonizing and ordering the patchwork of state and local regulatory regimes.

In the late twentieth century, firms operate in a global economy. Without a global political entity to restrain trade, to "harmonize" regulations, to create a "level playing field," special interests and ideological groups lack the means of restricting competition. The value of trade and the mobility of capital create the functional equivalent of the interstate commerce clause that protected internal trade in the United States before the railroads and Progressives managed to establish the ICC.

Today, economic interests (major multinational corporations) stressed by global competition join with ideological interests (a powerful environmental movement) to create the global equivalent of the Interstate Commerce Commission — an agency that could restrain trade to ensure that it is "sustainable."

None of the other Bretton Woods institutions — the World Bank, the IMF, the old GATT — can play this global cartelization role. Nor could the U.N. But the WTO might.

Like NAFTA, the WTO's merits will be determined by seemingly marginal details — in particular, the actions of its Committee on Trade and the Environment. Disturbing trends have already begun to emerge from NAFTA's side agreements. The Mexican operations of General Electric and Honeywell have been charged with violating NAFTA's labor laws, and both companies are now under investigation. Even if no formal disciplinary action is taken, these companies will have been forced to spend substantial sums in their defense, setting a grim example for other businesses. Mexico has already been pressured into adopting U.S.-style laws regarding food inspection and the transportation of hazardous wastes. And U.S. firms are being pressured to comply with U.S. toxic release inventory laws in Mexico, even though no law requires this as such.

If NAFTA could already do so much damage, do we really have nothing to fear from the WTO?

But even without these complexities, the WTO deserves scrutiny. It is a GATT with teeth, and those teeth can enable it to discipline protectionism. They can also enable it to enforce protectionism more effectively than ever before.

Mexican Hayride
by R. W. Bradford

"I've been madly buying Mexican stocks, currencies, and U.S. debt all day . . ." It was a hastily scrawled note faxed to me January 30 by a friend who earns his living as a speculator. On that day, the peso fell 10%, to new all-time lows, and Mexican stocks were collapsing. But my friend figured that the politicians and Wall Street types would prevail in the end, and bail out the Mexican government.

When the Mexican peso collapsed in mid-December, Bill Clinton promised Mexico a big pile of money. Not his money, of course. Our money. $40,000,000,000 of it. "But it's not like we're spending the money," he said. "It's like we're co-signing a note."

The bailout was needed, he explained, because Mexico is our biggest trading partner; if it has to default on its loans, it won't be able to finance future imports from the U.S. Furthermore, he said, if the peso falls more, the Mexican economy will be hit even harder, which will drive more Mexicans across the Rio Grande.

The American people understood Clinton's message all too well. They realized that when you co-sign a note, you have to pay up if the borrower defaults. The last time they recalled our government "co-signing a note" was less than a decade ago, when it guaranteed savings-and-loan deposits — a decision that ultimately cost hundreds of billions of dollars.

Furthermore, people wondered who would gain from such a bailout. Certainly not the people of Mexico, who will still suffer under the heel of a profligate government that spends most of its effort lining the pockets of wealthy Mexicans. The Mexican government always buys popular support with wild spending for a few months prior to each presidential election, only to have the United States — i.e., the American taxpayer — bail it out after the election. This is the third election in a row that was prefaced with a spending binge and followed by an American bailout.

So who really gained from the bailout? American investors who purchased Mexican bonds that otherwise would not be repaid, that's who. And why did American investors and institutions buy Mexican bonds rather than others? There's just one reason: Mexican bonds paid higher interest rates.

Of course, as with any investment, bigger payoffs are the product of bigger risks. In other words, the American investors who sent their money to Mañanaland *knew they were taking a bigger risk.*

During January, the Wall Street investors, banks, and institutions who had accepted that risk were busy lobbying Congress to cough up $40 billion for Mexico. They told us they were motivated by a desire to do good, to protect American jobs, to help poor Mexicans, to prevent an upswing in illegal immigration, etc. It was entirely an accident that the bailout would line their pockets.

The following day, Bill Clinton did what Congress wouldn't do: he bailed out Mexico using $20 billion from the U.S. Exchange Stabilization Fund (which is directly under his control, but had previously been thought unavailable for such bailouts), and getting the International Monetary Fund and the Bank for International Settlements to cough up another $30 billion.

And so the Mexican government can repeat its cycle of vote-buying and begging, Mexican peasants can continue to live under grinding poverty with a party thrown for them every six years, Wall Street investors can breath freely, and you and I can look forward to a loss of only $20 billion in taxpayer money, instead of the $40 billion Clinton originally proposed. And my friend made a fortune by serving the function of the speculator: taking big risks when others are afraid or cautious.

Letting the Market Work

All through the "crisis," Clinton, the Wall Street bankers, the Republican leadership,* and other advocates of the bailout issued dire warnings about the horrible consequences that would follow if the U.S. treasury isn't raided for the benefit of the Mexican government and its bondholders.

According to Lawrence Summers, Clinton's undersecretary of the Treasury for international affairs, the bailout had nothing to do with helping wealthy American investors:

> This is about promoting U.S. exports, about preventing illegal immigration into our country. Most importantly, this is about the kind of economic system that the U.S. has stood for since the Cold War ended: market-based capitalism. And if Mexico were allowed to encounter dire financial distress it would have reverberations around the world. You know you saw that yesterday when the Brazil stock market went down 8% on news about what was happening with respect to U.S. policy toward Mexico. You see that in political discussions in a variety of countries in Asia where the idea of open markets, the idea of economic liberalization is questioned because of concerns about what happened in Mexico.
>
> This has nothing to do with bailing out investors. This has to with protecting America's fundamental national interests.

In sum, according to Clinton's man, when the U.S. government bails out a bunch of wealthy investors and a profligate government, this amounts to a defense of "market-based capitalism."

But Summers didn't stop there.

> I'd sure have to disagree that the Latin American debt crisis of the 1980s was some kind of picnic. If you look at what happened, U.S. exports to Latin America fell by more than 50% during the period of the last debt crisis. Illegal immigration rose by more than a third.

---

* In an amazing press conference following the bailout, Newt Gingrich was beside himself with praise for Clinton's decision, asserting that it was "statesmanlike," "courageous," and worthy of Winston Churchill.

You know, in fact, in the three weeks since the peso collapsed, you see illegal immigration apprehensions on parts of our border rise threefold.

I think it's a view of yesterday's world to say that somehow financial distress in our neighbor has no real effect. We can make a difference. We have made a difference and it's very much in our national interest. That's why we're doing this.

We're sure of what would have happened if we had not been prepared to act, and it would not have been pretty. It would have made the kind of adjustment that Mexico's going to have to go through now much, much more serious. . . .

Will this work? Strong economic conditions in Mexico. Strong conditions on their borrowing, on their money, on their fiscal policy. A Mexican economy that's now based on the private sector in a way like it wasn't before. An up-front fee that Mexico is going to have to pay for any guarantees that we give them. Ultimate recourse to Mexico's oil export revenues. I think it will work. You know, that Chile thing, Chile went through a lot of hell, and it would have been a big problem for us in the early '80s if it had been on our border. But you know again, that's living in the past. In those days you had a small number of bank creditors and you could get them all together and you could push them to continue lending. You could work out a negotiated free-market solution. In today's world of thousands of creditors all dispersed, that's just not a possibility.

Before he began to babble incoherently, Summers mentioned that the loan will be secured by "Mexico's oil export revenues." Some security: the only way we can use that "ultimate recourse" for payment is the same way we can get them to repay now: by military invasion. Early in this century, the United States and other great powers did occasionally use their military to enforce repayment of loans. But that was before poor countries built modern armies. This alternative has been considered unacceptable for more than half a century.

Ironically, one of the first times the U.S. refused to use force to collect a debt occurred in 1938, when the government of Mexico expropriated American-owned oil companies, organizing the confiscated property into Pemex, the huge, grossly mismanaged, government-owned oil company whose revenue now will "secure" the new loans.*

Summers also mentioned Chile, which suffered a similar financial crisis in the early 1980s, differing mainly in that the United States government did not intervene with a huge pile of your money. Did the disaster that Summers seemed to be predicting occur?

Well, yes and no. In the short term, Chileans suffered. With their currency practically worthless, they couldn't afford to import much from abroad, and the standard of living in Chile declined sharply. But just as the collapse of Chile's currency made imports very expensive, its collapse made its exports cheap. Because of the crisis, Chile freed up its economy, reducing regulations and taxes. Today, a decade later, Chile has the most prosperous economy in Latin America and is setting an example for the "undeveloped" world. It has also, perhaps not coincidentally, embraced the sort of democratic reforms that Mexico seems incapable of adopting.

And what happened to the investors in Chilean bonds? They took their lumps, and they learned something about investing in countries that don't follow a sound financial policy.

Profit and loss play vital roles in the marketplace. When individuals invest their money or labor in a way that fills other people's needs, they make a profit. When they invest money or effort in ways that do not fill others' needs, they lose. If you protect people from risk of loss, you encourage them to invest in ways that do not serve other people, thereby undermining the whole economy.

Bankruptcy serves an important role in a market economy. It liquidates bad investments, sends signals to investors to put their

---

* Mexico considers this act of theft to be a great historical accomplishment. In 1988, Mexico celebrated the fiftieth anniversary of the event by issuing a set of commemorative gold coins. Needless to say, unlike other commemorative Mexican coins, these were not heavily promoted in the United States.

money in sounder ventures, and redistributes assets from incompetent managers to competent ones.

Of course, governments are not private enterprises. Free-market businesses deal with their customers on the basis of voluntary, mutual benefit: if you don't want to buy a good or service, you don't have to. Governments, by contrast, can force their "customers" (their citizens) to buy goods or services regardless of whether they want the "benefits" or not, and even to make payments without any good or service offered in return. If you don't believe me, try not paying your taxes.

Allowing a government to go bankrupt is even more important than allowing a business to go bankrupt, for it is the only way to discourage the profligacy of a government like the one Mexico suffers under today, or Chile suffered under prior to its crisis. In the long run, the very best thing the United States could have done for Mexico would have been to let it suffer the discipline of the international marketplace.

What happened after the $50 billion bailout? The peso rallied briefly, but then began to fall again. As I write these words, the peso is worth 13.5¢, down more than 15% from its level *before* the bailout. In other words, the precise disaster that Bill Clinton said would occur it we didn't bail out Mexico has occurred.

The U.S. dollar has collapsed with the peso, falling to its lowest level ever against the Japanese yen and the German mark. Today, it costs about 90 yen to buy one U.S. dollar. That same dollar bought you 235 yen in 1985. Today a German mark costs about 72¢. In 1985, you could buy that same mark for 29¢.

European speculators have concluded that the currency of a government willing to put billions on the line to help Mexico or Wall Street may not be a very good investment.

So far, Bill Clinton hasn't said a word about the calamitous post-bailout collapse of the peso. Apparently he has bigger things to worry about.

Hail to the Wimp!
by Leon T. Hadar

Many of my friends envy me for being a "Washington-based journalist." It sounds so romantic, so important! Sure, everyone knows reporters don't make much money, but working in the U.S. capital means the opportunity to mingle with the famous and powerful. People are always asking me questions: "Can you go to those White House press conferences? Do you get to see Clinton? How does Sam Donaldson look in person? Does he really wear a toupee?"

Well, to be honest with you, the last time I saw Donaldson was on ABC's *This Week*, and I prefer to watch White House press conferences from the comfort of my air-conditioned bedroom. In fact, *most* of my Washington reporting is done from the comfort of my air-conditioned bedroom. I begin my day reading the *New York Times*, the *Washington Post*, and *The Wall Street Journal*. Then I watch a bit of CNN and C-Span (and my favorite soap). I do some jogging, read the news wire reports on my on-line service, glance at the news releases I receive on my fax machine, or skim through the World Bank or Commerce Department reports delivered to me with your tax money (sucker!). And maybe, if I really feel in the mood, I make a few phone calls to my "sources." Then I recycle all the info I've collected over the day into a news story or "analysis" and wire it to my newspaper.

That's how I make my living. Really!

Okay — sometimes, when the weather is good or the illegal immigrant who cleans my apartment shows up, I go out and do some "reporting." This consists mainly of attending boring press conferences, think-tank "briefings," and embassy receptions. The rewards come in the form of free lunches, *hors d'oeuvres*, and other refreshments. I also get to "network" with colleagues, hoping to find a job that pays even more for this parasitic existence, and to flirt with some of the young chicks who flock to Washington.

One Friday, in the last week of July, I decided that it was time for me to take advantage of my press credentials and do some honest reporting. It was hot and humid in Washington, with very high levels of pollen, and the idea of having to wear a tie and jacket didn't seem very enticing. But when I heard that the diplomatic and national-security biggies of the Republican Party — former Secretary of State James "Jim" Baker, former Defense Secretary Richard "Dick" Cheney, former U.N. Ambassador Jeane "Jeane" Kirkpatrick, all-around statesman Henry "Doctor" Kissinger — would all be bashing Clinton at a foreign policy forum organized by the Republican National Committee, I just couldn't resist the temptation.

So I hopped into a non-air-conditioned cab, whose Nigerian driver took me to a K Street hotel. There I found one of those stuffy Washington foreign policy events where pompous media and think-tank types socialize and exchange ideas (and business cards).

I recalled attending similar gatherings in the glorious Reagan years, at the peak of the Cold War and the struggle against Soviet-sponsored terrorism, or during the video-game days of Desert Storm, as Bush's New World Order was evolving. Back then, there was a sense of excitement in the air. Here we were in the capital of the Free World, the New Rome, where Global History was being shaped, where the balance of power in "Euro-Asia" was being rearranged by the competent managers of Empire. And we were all part of it, extras in the great motion picture. It was a world where powerful and virile men of action, diplomats, strategists, and the female TV reporters who slept with them could make one hell of a global difference. Yeah! Those were the days.

Now, as I entered the hotel hall and observed the GOP contributors chewing the last morsels of their disgusting lunch and waiting for the proceedings to begin, I felt a sense of emptiness in the air. *Things ain't what they used to be,* I told myself. One look at the unemployed beltway bandits, causeless neocon writers, and retired global crusaders around me said it all. Here we are, close to the midterm point of the Clinton presidency, and America has yet to be engaged in any hot, lukewarm, or cold wars. Peace is breaking out all over. There's no Evil Empire to push around anymore, no anti-Communist military despots to prop up, no "freedom fighters" to support. Even the Israelis and Yasser Arafat are making peace — a major blow to the neocons, who are now trying to out-Zionize the Israeli government.

And the American people don't give a hoot about foreign policy. It's one of the last items on the list of concerns in the average American's mind, sandwiched somewhere between the fate of the spotted owl and the whereabouts of the space station. Typist-turned-CNN-correspondent Christina Amampour broadcasts from the roof of a bombarded Sarajevo building every night, trying to convince Americans to fight in Bosnia. To no avail. Despite all the efforts of U.S. television's British stringers to bombard us with horrible images of tortured, wounded, and dying Bosnians/Somalis/Azeris/Haitians, public support for sending troops to any of these hot spots is next to nil. Isolationism, bless it, is alive and well in our beloved post-Cold War America.

And who knows better than that infamous draft dodger, the wimp himself, Bill "Don't Get Killed, Get a Blow Job" Clinton? When it comes to foreign policy, this president is just my kind of guy.

Yes, I know he made all those promises during the campaign about how he was going to spread democracy around the globe, save the Bosnian Muslims, punish the tyrants in Beijing, and cleanse the Third World of nuclear weapons. Plus, he committed himself to the principles of "assertive multilateralism" — that is, following the U.N. to fight for democracy anywhere and anyplace on the planet.

We thought we were getting a new Woodrow Wilson, a moralist interventionist, an idealist statesman who would try to make the world safe for democracy. Instead, we got a Warren Harding, a pragmatic neo-isolationist, a corrupt politician who wants to make the world safe for business — kind of a global Arkansas.

I suspected all along that Clinton's internationalist rhetoric was little more than campaign baloney for the columnists and foreign policy "insiders." But it wasn't until I saw Clinton's foreign policy team on television that I knew that the Republic was safe. Did anyone seriously think that aging Warren Christopher, bookish Anthony Lake, and eccentric Les Aspin were going to lead America into war?

Now, even with the more energized William Perry at Defense, the foreign policy team looks and sounds like it's OD'd on Prozac. It's true, the president and his aides keep espousing that crap about the U.S. being the only remaining superpower in the world. But they've been generally faithful to their commitment to cut the defense budget, making it harder to achieve that sacred Pentagon goal, to fight on two fronts (say, in Korea and the Persian Gulf). And they seem to be making the right moves so as to make NATO and all the other Cold War dinosaurs obsolete.

Now imagine a Jack Kemp presidency, with its expanding military budgets and crusades for global democracy. See what I'm getting at?

In Somalia, the Clintonites, following their U.N. lead, invited a bloody shootout. But then they cut their losses and authored a new policy directive that forbids Washington to back up a new interventionist U.N. adventure. They even refused to characterize the slaughter in Rwanda as "genocide," so as not to create the legal basis for a major U.S. military intervention there.

Bosnia? As Pat Buchanan recently noted, the president "has threatened Bosnia's Serbs more times than Jackie Gleason's bus driver Ralph Kramden shook his fist in the face of wife Alice shouting, 'One of these days, Alice! Pow! Right on the kisser!'" But despite the pressure from the Left and the Right, from Bill Safire and Jim Hoagland and *The New Republic*, Clinton and his aides were able to brilliantly rationalize their more-or-less non-interventionist posture in the Balkans. Good for them!

I loved the way Clinton climbed down from a threat to impose sanctions on China and the way he reestablished trade ties with Hanoi. Did you notice how he had to go through all that agony of surrendering to the butchers of Tiananmen Square and giving up the idea of sending Rambo to find those missing servicemen in the Vietnam jungle? In the end — as always with this president — money talks. And thanks to this unprincipled White House steward, trade will flow more freely across the Pacific, making the Chinese, Vietnamese, and American people happier and more prosperous.

I'll admit I was a little concerned in Clinton's early days. I was afraid all the criticism coming from the foreign policy insiders ("Draft-dodger!" "Inexperienced!" "Wimp!") would force Clinton to get macho, to follow his predecessor's path to proving his manhood by bombing some Middle Eastern country into the stone age. Instead, our young president, in what seemed to be a mild form of ejaculation, dropped a few bombs on an "intelligence center" in Baghdad and left Saddam alone most of the time. I didn't care for that, but it's better than what Bush did.

Actually, Clinton's entire "Middle East policy" seems to consist of inviting leaders from the region to shake hands on the White House lawn and serving as an effective master of ceremonies. (I did attend Clinton's Arafat-Rabin handshake performance, and I can tell you: the guy is smooth.)

And Clinton was certainly a master strategist in the "North Korean crisis," sending Jimmy Carter to Pyongyang to buy some time and ignoring the advice of the Republican crazies. If it were up to *them*, we would already be in the middle of Korean War II, with Seoul nuked and tens of thousands of Americans and Koreans dead. Instead, Clinton took the advice of the Asians, which, more or less, was "Who needs a war now? We're doing so much business and making so much money in Asia. Let's wait for Kim Il Sung to die, and then maybe we'll be able to buy his playboy-midget son Kim Jong Il with a few bucks and yen." And what do you know? Kim Senior is dead, and it looks like Junior may be ready to cut a deal in return for a fresh supply of X-rated Swedish videos.

I'll admit I don't like Clinton's polices toward Haiti. As far as I'm concerned, it doesn't matter whether it's "Father" Aristide or bloody General Cedras who's leading the killing spree in Port-Au-Prince. If it were up to me, I would have lifted the embargo on that poor island yesterday and allowed all those hard-working Haitians to immigrate to Miami, thereby diluting the power of the Cuba lobby.

Still, isn't it refreshing to see a president making it clear to everyone that he's ready to send American soldiers to their deaths in Haiti, not to preserve Western civilization and the Judeo-Christian way of life, but to maintain the Congressional Black Caucus' support for his health package? (Public Choice economists could come up with an interesting model correlating the number of American war casualties and Congressional votes on the health-care bill, graphed nicely as indifference curves.)

So, since it looks like the only major foreign policy excitement we're apt to get during the Clinton term is a splendid little war in Haiti, it is not surprising that Washington's international-ist set is so depressed — which brings me back to that Republican foreign policy forum in Washington. As I mentioned before, that event forced me to leave my cool apartment on a muggy July day. You are all probably asking: *Was it worth it, Leon?* I could've spent that time at the pool, or taking a long afternoon nap, or watching *Sonya Live* or *Oprah*. Instead, I had to sit through frustrated right-wing Cold Warriors explaining why they should be back in power, so they can make American foreign policy "credible" again and turn Washington back into a safe sanctuary for the veteran managers of the National Security State, for the Global Democracy buffs, for the demented unipolarists.

I certainly didn't get any story from the event, unless you want to count this one. My newspaper doesn't even come out on Saturday. But I did learn a lot, and came to some provocative conclusions.

When "Jim" and "Dick" and "Jeane" and "Dr. Kissinger" say it isn't in America's "national interest" to invade Haiti, the not-so-subtle message to the white middle-class voters is, *Do you really want to see American boys* (and girls — sorry!) *die for the sake of a bunch of AIDS-stricken niggers?* I believe that fighting a war in Haiti is not in anyone's interest. But Kirkpatrick and her neocon buddies tell us that it is in America's "national interest" to help the westernized yuppies of Sarajevo. Cheney and his Pentagon pals explain that it is in our "national interest" to send more money to the military, the CIA, and the rest of the National Security State apparatus. Baker wants to see a rerun of the Gulf War on the Korean Peninsula — again, that "national interest."

Kissinger believes that we should be doing our best to expand NATO and prepare it to deal with the new "threats": Islamic fundamentalism, Russian nationalism, etc., etc. And of course, all the great Republican foreign policy strategists think it's in America's "national interest" to continue its huge entitlement program for Israel and its security services for the Saudi royal family, and to prepare for a great war against the ayatollahs in Teheran, whom they see as a threat to Israel and the oil sheiks. (In other words, what's good for Israel and the oil lobby is good for America.)

Which leads me to the following question, which I'd like to pose to you, the thinking libertarian: Who would you really prefer to see presiding in Washington after 1996? Hilarious Hillary and Horny Bill, trying (unsuccessfully) to get all their big government domestic programs passed by Congress, visiting our vacationing troops in sunny Haiti, drowning in the Whitewater, and constantly providing us with ammunition to use against the political class? Or deadly serious President Dick Cheney, his "virtuous" wife Lynn, and their company of wild-eyed spooks, military adventurers, and neocon *Commentary* propagandists, presiding over Gulf War II, Korean War III, Cold War IV, Iran-Contra V, and Watergate VI — while being forced by a Democratic Congress to pass all those big government programs anyway? Well?

Contrary to Republican propaganda, Clinton's poll ratings are falling, not because of his inability to handle foreign policy, but because he is incompetent, sleazy, and corrupt. In fact, the only reason he's still a serious contender for 1996 may be that he's kept the country at peace for close to two years. So I hope that Clinton will adopt Ron Paul's proposal to run under the "He Kept Us Out of War" banner in '96. And that he wins.

He may not get our votes, but he does deserve our sympathy.

Whitewater Was No Aberration

by R. W. Bradford

Initially, Bill and Hillary Clinton routinely responded to questions about their involvement with Whitewater Development and the failure of Madison Guaranty by angrily saying, "We haven't been accused of doing anything wrong." This was a lie, of course: already, the Clintons stood accused of violating the public trust, of looting the public treasury, of obstructing justice to cover their tracks, and of interfering with the investigation of a related death.

The pattern of corruption that has characterized the careers of the Clintons and their associates is far more extensive than can be summarized here. But here are some of the more interesting charges, and a brief summary of the evidence that supports them. I make no attempt even to hint at the pervasive evidence of their political and business allies' broader pattern of profiteering at taxpayer expense while skating on the edge of the law.

While governor of Arkansas, Bill Clinton neglected to enforce the law against a man who was the business partner of him and his wife. James ("Diamond Jim") McDougal, a long-time political colleague of the Clintons, purchased Morgan Guaranty Savings & Loan in 1982. He expanded its deposit base aggressively, in the process greatly increasing its loans to Arkansas politicians and officers of the bank. It was soon in financial trouble, thanks in part to bad loans to officers, friends of officers, and politicians, including a loan of $1,000,000 to then-Governor Jim Guy Tucker, half of which was written off.

Times may have been hard at Madison, but in January 1985, McDougal managed to hold a fundraiser for his old friend Bill Clinton in the lobby of the bank, raising money to help Bill pay back a bank loan used to finance the campaign that won back the governorship. At least one of the people who was recorded as a donor (coughing up a $3,000 cashiers' check drawn on Madison) doesn't remember ever making the donation, while other donors, employees of Madison, made their contributions with the understanding that McDougal would pay them back.

Meanwhile, regulators were about to close down Madison because of insufficient capital. McDougal decided the way to keep Madison open was to raise capital by selling stock. But there was a problem: it isn't easy to get regulatory approval to sell stock in failing financial institutions. McDougal put his old friend Hillary Rodham Clinton of the Rose Law Firm on retainer as attorney for Madison. Bill Clinton, at the recommendation of McDougal, appointed Beverly Bassett Schaffer to be his new banking regulator; Ms. Schaffer had previously served as attorney for Madison. Then Ms. Clinton, representing Madison, requested Schaffer's approval of the stock offering. One of the supporting documents provided by Ms. Clinton was a favorable review of the S&L's condition by Frost & Co., its accountants. The head auditor on the project was James Alford, who had two outstanding loans from Madison that neither he nor Ms. Clinton disclosed.

Schaffer approved the stock offering. Madison stayed open and continued to make extremely risky loans to its officers. In February 1986, for example, it lent $672,000 to Judge David Hale. In March, Hale lent McDougal's wife $300,000 of federal money earmarked for loans to minorities. McDougal used $100,000 of that money to shore up Whitewater, the corporation that the McDougals and Clintons started in 1978, when Clinton was attorney general. It looked like a pretty good deal for the Clintons, who received half ownership but didn't have to put up much money. But things hadn't worked out and it needed cash. Hale never paid back the $672,000 he borrowed from Madison, and McDougal never paid back the $300,000 loan from the government. In October 1986, McDougal was ousted as chairman of

Madison.

Madison didn't go belly-up until March 1989, when federal regulators took it over and tried to make some sense of the whole mess. Vincent Foster, Jr., one of Ms. Clinton's law partners, offered his services on behalf of the federal government without bothering to mention that his firm had previously been attorney for Madison. The firm got the job. The attorney that the firm assigned to the case was Webster Hubbell. He sued Frost & Co, the accounting firm that had issued Madison a clean bill of health, for $60 million, the amount of the government's loss in the failure of Madison, but settled the suit for $1 million, reportedly about half the sum payable by Frost's insurance company. Ms. Clinton's law firm got $400,000 of this settlement as its fee for handling the negotiations. The resolution of the situation let a number of debtors off the hook, including Seth Ward, Hubbell's father-in-law, who got out of repaying a debt of $573,793.

All that the Clintons appear to have got out of the deal was the money raised by McDougal, the fees directed to the Rose Law Firm, and their investment in Whitewater Development. Although Whitewater turned out to be a loser, it actually profited the Clintons. It seems that as investors, the Clintons were never asked to put up much money, though they stood to make very large profits if the project worked. As it was, they made a modest gain by deducting from their income tax certain interest paid by Whitewater. Unhappily for the Clintons, the law doesn't let you deduct expenses you never paid, and when the Whitewater matter came under public scrutiny, they paid up. What had started as a risk-free prospective gold mine for the Clintons ended up a tax fraud that would have worked had not the Whitewater-Madison mess come under scrutiny in the wake of Clinton's election.

There were no criminal investigations. The whole episode fell under the rubric of business as usual, just another corrupt deal in the nation's most corrupt state — but not that different from cor-

rupt deals involving scheming businessmen, government regulators, and the public treasury everywhere else in the country. If
Bill Clinton had not been elected president, the whole matter
would have been forgotten. But Bill Clinton *was* elected president, in part on a campaign to clean up government. Those who
knew of his activities in Arkansas were annoyed by his hypocrisy, and they raised the issue publicly.

Then, on July 20, 1994, a bullet entered the head of Vincent
Foster, the Clintons' personal attorney, Hillary's former law
partner and reputed lover, a man deeply involved in the investigation of irregularities concerning Madison Guaranty and
Whitewater Development. Foster's death was reported as a suicide, though many independent investigators have raised the possibility of murder. The investigation of his death was peculiar, to
say the least. For one thing, police investigating the case were
denied access to his office while Clinton aides removed personal
and business documents. Among the items removed was a brief-
case containing a torn-up note, written in Foster's hand, describ-
ing his distraught mental state. Curiously, the note was
"overlooked" at the time, and even after it was noticed, Clintons'
aides waited 30 hours before turning it over to the police.

The circumstances of Foster's death may never be known.
But it is undeniable that the Clintons interfered with its investigation. The net effect of the Foster death was to cast ugly suspicions on the Clintons, suspicions they could have avoided by not
removing evidence from his office and by allowing a proper
investigation of his death by competent authorities.

In sum, there is no doubt that the Clintons violated the public
trust by failing to reveal conflicts between their own private
financial interests and the public interest, and there are consider-
able indications that they looted the public treasury by a number
of fraudulent subterfuges. It is possible, I suppose, that Hillary
Clinton's opposition to investigating the Whitewater-Madison
affair was motivated by considerations other than fear of appre-

hension. But how else can one explain the fact that when a special prosecutor was appointed to investigate the matter, and the possibility of a subpoena of records relevant to the case became a real possibility, the Rose Law Firm immediately began shredding Foster's files? How else can one explain the Clintons' interference with the investigation of the Foster's death?

Whitewater said quite a bit about Clintonism. Here, for the whole world to see, was a real "public-private partnership" in action.

Whitewater and Watergate

Supporters of the Clintons attempted to dismiss the whole scandal as a partisan attempt by Republicans to do personal harm to the Clintons and divert the public's attention from the White House's legislative agenda. Meanwhile, Republicans persisted in their curiosity and their criticisms, even comparing Whitewater to the infamous Watergate scandal that brought down the Nixon presidency 20 years ago. Apparently, Republicans are oblivious to the obvious point that by comparing the Clintons' problems to Richard Nixon's, they are accusing the Democrats of being as corrupt as a Republican.*

Just how similar are the Clinton scandals and Watergate? Apologists for the Clintons typically see Watergate as far more serious than the Whitewater charges. Typical is the view of Sam Dash, former counsel for the Senate Watergate Committee, as quoted by *The Wall Street Journal*:

> The only thing that Whitewater has in common with Watergate is "water."

---

* I am reminded of a contest sponsored by the *Baltimore Sun*, in which readers were invited to answer the question, "What's the difference between a Republican and a Democrat?" The winning entry: "A Republican is a person who believes the Democrats are ruining the country. A Democrat is a person who believes the Republicans are ruining the country. (Both of them are right.)"

> Watergate involved a president, Richard Nixon, who committed serious crimes in office solely to advance his political ambitions. Perhaps at no other time has our constitutional democracy been more in danger.
>
> It is really nonsensical to compare these crimes with the undefined allegations relating to Whitewater [which] involved commercial transactions that may have been engaged in by Bill and Hillary Clinton years before he was elected president.

This may be the way most Americans see things today — though I believe they will change their view of things as the complexities of the case unravel — but it's not the way I see it.

The burglary of the Democratic Party's headquarters and subsequent attempts to cover up the presidential campaign's involvement seems to me to be pretty much the sort of shenanigans that politicians habitually play. I can recall a Democratic "prankster" who appeared on the Johnny Carson show to brag about his efforts to sabotage Republican campaigns. The whole business was considered funny. I remember stories about how John F. Kennedy's grandfather had his campaign workers telephone uncommitted voters in the middle of the night posing as campaign aides for his opponent, a tactic which was also considered to be clever and amusing. Snooping into an opponent's campaign plans doesn't seem a lot different.

Say what you like about Nixon, but the Watergate crimes occurred entirely within the context of the political game. His actions were aimed at his opponent and their actions were aimed at him. He cheated at the game, was caught, and tried to weasel his way out of it. The money used to finance the break-in and try to cover it up came from campaign contributions, not the taxpayer. Politics is a game with only one real rule: anything that gets you elected is okay, unless you're tossed out of office and into jail.

In the end, Nixon lost the game, barely escaping the hoosegow. The effects of his actions on the government and on the American people were relatively minor, and virtually all good:

he disgraced the office of the presidency and shook people's confidence in government. So what's the big deal?

We may figure spitballer Gaylord Perry was a cheater at baseball and that Bill Laimbeer was a dirty basketball player, but we aren't about to put either on trial in public courts for their failure to play by the rules of their games. The same was true, more or less, of Nixon, the Watergate break-in, and its subsequent cover-up — except that his opposing team controlled the officiating.

In contrast, the Clintons are accused of fraud against the United States Treasury, of being paid accomplices in the looting of a savings and loan association, that cost the taxpayers approximately $60 million. Furthermore, they stand accused of obstructing justice by destroying documentary evidence that might be used against them. And they are charged with intervening in the investigation of the death of an individual deeply involved in the fraud.

Whether anyone will ever get to the bottom of these charges remains to be seen. The president, after all, is the most powerful person in the world. He is in charge of the very police agencies responsible for investigating his apparent crimes, and appointed the very prosecutor responsible to bring legal action against him. Furthermore, the fraud perpetrated by the Clintons and their cronies is extremely complex; many people lack either the inclination or the intellect to understand it.

Until late February of 1994, most of the American media trod very lightly. The media boycott of the story reached such a point that *The Economist*, the rather staid British newsweekly, speculated in its February 26 issue that there might be a "conspiracy of silence" regarding the Clintons' shenanigans. *The Economist* compared the situation in America today to that in Britain in 1937, when the British media blacked out all coverage of the constitutional crisis occasioned by the new king's affair with a divorced American, an affair that led to his abdication and exile.

Just as Britishers who wanted information about that constitutional crisis had to read foreign newspapers, so many Americans have had to go to the foreign press for details of the Whitewater scandal. *The Economist* illustrated this story with photocopies of coverage of the Clinton crisis from the British press. "House of Secrets" ran one headline, over a photograph of the White House. "Big Trouble at Little Rock" ran another, over a photo of Hillary Rodham Clinton. "Suicide or Murder?" ran a third, over a photo of Vince Foster, thereby touching a subject of much speculation and suspicion everywhere in America except the major media.

The media blackout fell apart on February 24, when Roger Altman, acting head of the Resolution Trust Corporation, admitted in congressional testimony that he had briefed the Clintons' staff on the status of the RTC investigation of the Madison Guaranty scandal. The RTC is supposedly a completely independent agency, and the fact that it briefed the staff of individuals under investigation was too scandalous for even the *New York Times* to ignore. Altman's revelation touched off a maelstrom of major-media interest. Within a few days, ABC News was referring to the Clinton administration as a "moral swamp" and even *Newsweek* was having second thoughts about the heroic character of the first lady.

By early March of 1994, the Clintons appeared to be on the edge of paranoia. A March 12 Associated Press dispatch from Detroit described how the president responded to questions about the scandal:

> Shifting to the edge of his seat, visibly agitated and eyes bulging, the president wagged his finger at two reporters and unleashed a rising torrent of complaint. . . .
>
> As he stood to end the interview, Clinton was asked if he would make public his tax returns from 1978 and 1979, which could reveal information about his investment in the Whitewater real estate deal in Arkansas at the root of the controversy.
>
> Clinton's face reddened in anger as he argued that he has given

all relevant financial records to independent counsel Robert Fiske and that legal procedure now prohibits him from releasing the records to the public.

Calmer heads among his remaining advisors tried to discourage further outbursts of this sort. Less than two weeks later, Clinton had regained his self-control and told a press conference that he was making public the same tax returns that had precipitated his Detroit tantrum. Apparently, the "legal procedure" he had cited in Michigan no longer applied. The similarity between Clinton's angry, near-panicky behavior and that of Nixon in his final days is eerie.

Spinning Out of Control

The Clintons acted quickly to attempt to reassert control of the situation. First, they ordered the resignation of White House Counsel Bernard Nussbaum, in hopes that offering a sacrificial goat would quiet the outraged public and put the awakened press back to sleep. Then they made a big show of ordering all White House personnel to comply fully with subpoenas issued by special prosecutor Robert Fiske, as if their minions might be thinking about committing perjury on behalf of the Clintons. Then they put their spin doctors on overtime.

For example . . . on March 30, 1994, David Gergen (then "counselor" to President Clinton) appeared as a guest on a C-Span call-in program, ostensibly to discuss his career as a journalist, but offering surprising evidence about how the Clinton administration hoped to divert public attention from Whitewater. Apropos of nothing, after responding to what the host had said was the final question, Gergen gave the following monologue:

> I just want to come back to one thing, look, since this is the last call. Ah, these issues are difficult, I know, for a lot of us to sort out. And I don't think anyone in the White House staff can claim to have absolute knowledge of any of this. We simply don't have time, nor is it appropriate for us to go back, and as a member of the staff, and look at 14,000 pages of documents about that was started

16 or 17 years ago, whatever the number of years ago are.

What I do think is important is that the president has set up a process — he's been involved in full disclosure — and we go forward on Whitewater. And the same time, I think what's very important is that we go forward with the rest of the nation's agenda. And, you know, some of us may agree or disagree about what the president's particular proposals are. You know I've come into an administration where I don't always find myself in agreement with my colleagues, naturally enough. I come out of a different, you know, political tradition coming into this White House. They, they asked me to come in. I've tried to be, I've tried to be as straightforward and honest about that as possible. Ah, but the critical thing is not whether I agree — any one of us disagrees — about a particular proposal. The critical thing is about whether we come together and get a move on these things. We cannot sit here as a country for the next three or four years and be so preoccupied with Watergate, with Whitewater, that we don't deal with these other issues. Let's deal with Whitewater. Let's be serious about it, upfront about it, involve full disclosure, but in the meantime let's get on with dealing about the way people live in their homes, let's get on with the crime program, let's get on with education, let's get on with welfare, and let's get on with health care reform.

Gergen gave the appearance of speaking extemporaneously, but during the 93 seconds it took to say those 346 words, he consulted his notes 23 times. Prior to this point, he spoke directly into the camera, without looking down at his papers. So it seems safe to conclude that here was a conscious, planned attempt to put a particular spin on recent events.

Let's examine what he said more closely, and see what impressions he was trying to create.

(1) *Whitewater is very complicated and confusing for "people like us" to understand, involving thousands of pages of documents about events that took place a long time ago.* The spin here is the implicit suggestion that these events are not very important, since they happened so long ago and are very complicated. Gergen neglected to mention that white-collar frauds are almost always complicated, and that most people care whether the president has stolen from the taxpayers, even if he did so

some years ago.

(2) *What's important is that Clinton is responding to all questions with a policy of "full disclosure."* Although Gergen figures Clinton's "full disclosure" is so important that he mentioned it twice, he didn't mention that Clinton resisted congressional inquiries and refused for months to appoint a special counsel to investigate Whitewater. Nor did he mention that Clinton's policy of "full disclosure" applies only to responding to subpoenas.

(3) *Gergen himself can't vouch for Clinton, but the issues are very complicated, and it's not his job to understand them, and anyway he is an independent who doesn't necessarily agree with others on the White House staff.* Here Gergen was protecting himself from future fallout from Whitewater — and inadvertently revealing that he fears Whitewater will at least seriously wound the Clinton administration. (Eventually, of course, Gergen did indeed flee his White House job.)

(4) *The country's priority should not be Whitewater, but rather the "nation's agenda: dealing about the way people live in their homes . . . the crime program . . . education . . . welfare, and . . . health care reform."* The issues that Gergen said the country and the president should focus on are Clinton's legislative agenda. Curiously, four items on that agenda — crime, education, health care, and welfare — are traditional responsibilities of the private sector and of state and local governments. And I don't know about you, but personally, I was not convinced that I ought to quit worrying about Whitewater and get back to the "nation's agenda," especially if one of the issues is "the way people live in their homes," the other item Gergen said deserves our attention.

And isn't it interesting that Gergen slipped and said "Watergate" instead of "Whitewater"?

Teatime With Hillary

Sometimes the Clintons took the job of spin-doctoring onto their own shoulders. Consider Hillary Clinton's April 22, 1994 press conference — a delightfully dramatic exercise intended to allay public suspicions about her wildly successful commodity trades in the late '70s, when she turned $1,000 into $100,000 in ten months' time. This spectacular performance is roughly similar to an unknown rookie baseball player batting .400 with 50 home runs and 150 runs batted in — and then retiring.

Needless to say, her spectacular profits raised some questions. Did she receive favorable treatment? If so, was this treatment the reward for some favor by her husband? And why had she hidden her spectacular record as a commodity trader from the public for more than a decade?

What Ms. Clinton said in her press conference is of only marginal interest, because she systematically avoided answering questions or providing any new information. But *how* she said it is fascinating. She constantly sought to give the *impression* that she was open about the whole business, saying things like "I'm glad you asked that" and maintaining perfect eye contact with reporters even as she evaded answering their questions.

She portrayed an entirely new character at her press conference. Instead of the take-charge, savvy, business-like feminist role-model co-president she had hitherto presented the public, she played the role of Mrs. Bill Clinton, wife and mother. Instead of standing in a power pose behind a lectern, Hillary sat on a dining room chair. Instead of her usual dress-for-success outfit, she wore a pretty pink sweater and skirt reminiscent of Pat Nixon. Instead of discussing "the president," she referred to "my husband." She was feminine, not feminist.

When asked substantive questions about her trading, she evaded, changed the subject, or claimed an inability to remember. She had no recollection of how she made a $5,300 profit on a $1,000 investment in a single day. She had no idea why she hadn't been subjected to margin calls. Through all her evasions and obfuscations, she never once lost her demeanor of housewifely openness. It was a brilliant performance.

At times, the sharp lawyer could be detected ("there's really no evidence of that," "I had no reason to believe that," "to the best of my recollection"). But even when reverting to cover-your-ass legalese she kept up her ingenuous style. Without providing a scintilla of explanation of how she had made such spectacular profits despite her lack of knowledge or experience, she feigned ignorance of even a clue to why a governor's wife might receive favorable treatment from a firm that happens to need relief from state regulation.

She did sneak in one obvious lie, but no one in the press noticed it. When asked why she made such a risky investment, she replied, "I didn't think it was that big a risk." At the time she contracted for liabilities of about $3,500,000, she had a net worth of about $60,000. Surely, she could not have believed that this "wasn't that big a risk." It may be that some naïve investors don't understand the risks involved in commodity futures contracts. But Hillary was a practicing attorney, a graduate of Yale Law School. Certainly, she cannot claim she hadn't bothered to read the fine print.

She did speak directly to one issue. Why had Bill and Hillary denounced the Reagan years as "a Gilded Age of greed and self-ishness, of irresponsibility and excess and of neglect" in which too many focused on "acquiring — acquiring wealth, power, privilege," when she and her husband had profited spectacularly from their own efforts to acquire great wealth in highly leveraged and risky transactions? The answer, she explained, was that she was imbued with traditional American virtues of thrift, providence, and a desire to provide a college education for her daughter, who at that point was just a gleam in her father's eye.

Most observers from the press thought she was a smashing success. She had managed to allay people's suspicions. As Howard Fineman of *Newsweek* put it, "This was a masterful piece of political theatre. I think it should go in the archive of every politician under pressure, who wants some instruction on how to seem calm and candid in the face of a lot of questions. She looked for all the world like someone who had nothing to hide."

It was the ultimate victory of form over substance. What is important in American public life is not honesty, but the *appearance* of honesty. What is important is not openness, but the *appearance* of openness. What is important is not integrity, but the *appearance* of integrity.

By changing her clothes, by adopting an ingenuous attitude, by sitting on an effeminate-looking chair, by feigning old-fashioned virtues, by looking people straight in the eye, by staying calm and collected, by acting the role of a submissive housewife shepherding her family's meager resources so they can avoid becoming a public charge in their nonage, she managed to deflect questions as artfully as any political spin doctor, and to portray herself as an entirely innocent victim of a nasty press and partisan opponents.

The Road to the Big House

Eventually, it all came crashing down for Hillary. Her role in the Whitewater scandals and the previously little-regarded Travelgate affair became harder and harder to cover up in early 1996, when she was caught in one lie after another.

For example: on April 6, 1994, Hillary Rodham Clinton responded to questions from the General Accounting Office about her role in firing the White House travel staff in early 1993 and replacing it with one consisting of relatives and political cronies. She had White House Counsel W. Neil Eggleston respond in these words: "Mrs. Clinton did not direct any action to be taken with regard to the Travel Office. Mrs. Clinton does not know the origins of the decision to remove the White House Travel Office employees. She believes that the decision to terminate the employees would have been made by Mr. Watkins with the approval of Mr. McLarty. Mrs. Clinton was aware that Mr.

Watkins was undertaking a review of the situation in the travel office, but she had no role in the decision to terminate the employees."

Virtually every word of that response was a lie, according to evidence the White House reluctantly released on January 3, 1996 to a House Committee investigating the matter. The same David Watkins who Mrs. Clinton had claimed made the decision entirely by himself with no direction from her, wrote a memo to Clinton Chief of Staff Mack McLarty, explaining that he fired the staff at "the First Lady's . . . insistence that the situation be resolved by replacing the Travel Office staff." Furthermore, Watkins added, he had made this decision out of fear of losing his job: "If I thought I could have resisted those pressures, undertaken more considered action, and remained in the White House, I certainly would have done so." The memo, designed to "set the record straight" (i.e., protect Watkins from prosecution), included a frank admission that he had "been as protective and vague as possible" in dealing with investigators.

Further evidence that Mrs. Clinton had lied came out a week later, with the release of a 1993 note written by White House aide Lorraine Volz: "Susan Thomases went to David and Mac [McLarty]. Hillary wants these people fired. Mac wouldn't do it. DW [David Watkins] didn't want to do it." When asked about these notes, Volz told *ABC News* that she "doesn't remember these notes exactly . . . but she cautioned that she was speaking to a reporter at the time, and these could be notes she was taking from that reporter." Right. She was being interviewed by a reporter, but she was taking notes on what the reporter said.

Mrs. Clinton responded to this new flurry of evidence by reiterating her story in what Ted Koppel called an "over-lawyerly" fashion:

> Well, I think what is fair to say is that I did voice concern about the financial mismanagement that was discovered when the president arrived here. In the White House travel office. I think that everyone

who knew about it was quite concerned and wanted it taken care of. But I did not make the decisions. I did not direct anybody to make the decisions. But I have absolutely no doubt that I did express concern, because I was concerned about any kind of financial mismanagement.

In other words, she didn't have them fired, and if she did, they deserved it. It is worth noting in passing that the White House had the head of the travel office put on trial for financial mismanagement. He was quickly acquitted and, along with all the other "financial mismanagers," given his job back with back pay.

Watkins' memo also included two other provocative passages. One mentions that "Vincent Foster became involved," but provides no details. Another makes a mysterious reference to the Secret Service: "an incident developed between the Secret Service and the First Family in February and March requiring resolution and action on your's [sic] and my parts. The First Family was anxious to have that situation immediately resolved, and the First Lady in particular was extremely upset with the delayed action in that case . . . after the Secret Service incident, it was made clear that I must move more forcefully and immediately follow the direction of the First Family."

The other document released on that evening was even more intriguing. Presidential Assistant Todd Stern speculated about how the media might react if the Travel Office firings were investigated:

> We need to think seriously about whether or not it won't be better to come clean, even to [the] point of conceding that HRC [Hillary Rodham Clinton] had some interest. . . . You risk merely compounding the problem by getting caught in half-truths. You run [the] risk of turning this into a "coverup."

Now we know that, prior to her deceiving the GAO and Congress and the public about the firings, Mrs. Clinton had been warned by a White House aide about the possibility — even the likelihood — that evasion or deception had tremendous risks.

Mrs. Clinton's decision to deceive was not made on the spur of the moment. It was made after careful consideration.

All this leads any intelligent person to wonder: *Just how much is she hiding?*

Two days later, a low-level White House employee found 115 pages of Rose Law Firm documents and billing records that provided substantial evidence of another systematic attempt by Mrs. Clinton to deceive authorities and the public about her involvement in Whitewater.

Remember, from the start of the inquiry into the Whitewater/ Madison Guaranty mess, Mrs. Clinton had systematically minimized any role she herself had played in the whole business. "There was a very bright young associate in our law firm who had a relationship with one of the officers at Madison," she said in her pretty-in-pink press conference. "The young attorney, the young bank officer, did all the work."

Well, not quite *all* the work. It turns out that Mrs. Clinton did quite a lot of the work herself. For example, she billed Madison for more than a dozen conferences with her partner Webb Hubbell's father-in-law, who borrowed $4 million from Madison that he never paid back. (*You* paid it back, you and America's other taxpayers. In all, you paid back $60 million borrowed from the bank owned by the Clintons' business partner and advised by Mrs. Clinton.) She also reviewed several documents, was involved in numerous conferences, and negotiated with the state's securities commissioner, who had been appointed to her job by Mrs. Clinton's husband. She also worked on a transaction involving a trailer park known as Castle Grande, which investigators suspect was part of the overall scheme to defraud the taxpayers. Last May, she told investigators for the Resolution Trust Corporation, "I don't believe I knew anything about" Castle Grande, and she told an FDIC investigator that she "was asked about a sewer project undertaken by Castle Grande." She replied that she was familiar with the name but had no other knowledge of the matter. The billing records show that she reviewed a twelve-page memo on the sewer project. Meanwhile, her personal attorney, David Kendall, continues to deny that she was in any way involved.

Curiously, the records had been annotated in red ink by Vincent Foster, Mrs. Clinton's close friend and law partner — and the First Family's damage control attorney — prior to his mysterious death in the summer of 1993.

It is also curious that the documents were discovered in the White House less than a week after the Resolution Trust Corporation had concluded its investigation into the Madison Guaranty business and decided not to prosecute the Clintons for lack of evidence.

And what of the "young attorney" Mrs. Clinton told the nation had done "all the work" regarding Madison Guaranty? He was Rick Massey, then with the firm for only eight months. From a note written in 1992 by Susan Thomases: "Rick will say he had a relationship with Latham and had a lot to do with getting the client in."

Old-Style Corruption

And on and on it goes. By the time this book is in print, there will no doubt be further revelations for the president and his wife to contend with. What is important here is not just the damage the scandal is doing to the Clintons, but the inevitability of such scandals. Like Watergate, the Whitewater-Madison mess is a strange throwback to the nineteenth century, when the political culture and the dominant styles of corruption in America were different than they are today.

"Power tends to corrupt, and absolute power corrupts absolutely." When Lord Acton made his famous observation 107 years ago, its underlying truth was well-recognized. Over the previous two centuries, the absolute power of Britain's monarchy had been replaced by the limited power of Parliament.

Although absolutism had never taken root in America, the truth of Acton's maxim was well appreciated on this side of the Atlantic. It underlay the American tradition of limited government. Government may be a "necessary evil" (in Thomas Paine's words), but restricting its scope and power could minimize its evil.

Binding government in Jefferson's "chains of the Constitution" did not prevent corruption; it only limited corruption within fairly specific boundaries. Cities, states, and the almost powerless federal government were in the hands of politicians, a class of individuals almost universally held in contempt by decent people.

Politicians created "machines" to insure their re-election and the election of allies. They lined their pockets and financed their campaigns with kickbacks from government contractors. Government jobs were rewards to the party faithful, who dutifully worked on the election campaigns of their bosses and often kicked back part of their salaries.

Corrupt deals were pretty much like any bargain among criminals: they were negotiated and explicitly agreed upon. The only difference between such agreements and legitimate business deals was that they could not be enforced by the courts. As a consequence, politicians, like criminals (one is tempted to say *other* criminals) depended on other means of enforcing contracts, primarily the expectation of profits from future deals and fear of retribution.

When the mayor wanted a kickback from the firm to whom he awarded the contract to build the new city hall, he negotiated with the contractor for a flat fee or percentage. If the contractor didn't pay the agreed-upon amount, the mayor would refuse him future business and perhaps have his police interfere with his ongoing operations.

Transactions between politicians had the same characteristic. The political boss of a large city might agree to deliver votes to a particular candidate for governor, in exchange for that governor allowing the political boss to name certain judges or control a particular government contract. The arrangement between a boss and his underling worked the same way: the party worker would agree to organize a precinct and deliver votes for the boss, and the boss would agree to give the party worker a specific government job.

The system worked reasonably well because everyone involved in a corrupt deal was a member of one or another of the political organizations or corrupt enterprises involved, and therefore depended on the enterprise for his job and income.

Perfecting Corruption

The apogee of this system was achieved in Louisiana in the 1930s under Huey Long, an immensely popular demagogue. As a precondition of employment, Long insisted that all his underlings tender an signed, undated letter of resignation. This condition applied to every single politician and employee of the State of Louisiana, from grade-school janitor to U.S. senator, giving Long the most control over government and politics of anyone in American history. Those who failed to toe the line could be threatened not only with loss of job and livelihood, but also with investigation, conviction, and imprisonment at the hands of policemen, district attorneys, judges, and prison officials under his absolute control.

When Long challenged Franklin Roosevelt's welfare programs with his own "Share Our Wealth" agenda, FDR used all the resources of the federal government to remove Long as a political rival. Long's system was so perfect that the vast power of the federal government could not harm him. But the system had a single weakness, exploited by Dr. Carl Weiss on September 8, 1936, who evaded Long's praetorian state troopers and put a fatal slug in the governor's gut before falling in a hail of bullets.

Long was corrupted by lust for power, not money. But his

carefully crafted system outlived him, and his successors' interests ran more toward cash. Thumbing their noses at federal investigators, they took the sensible precaution of making sure that all payoffs and bribes took the form of cash sent by railway express (to insulate themselves from mail fraud charges), and within a few years they were living in mansions with solid-gold toilet fixtures. With prosperity came laziness, and the Long empire fell when they allowed a bribe to be paid by check — which cleared through the mail.

But the Long machine was the exception, made possible by Long's extraordinary popularity, skill, and determination. No other political machine in America before or since has achieved such absolute control. Consequently, they have been vulnerable to less radical challenges than the assassin's bullet.

The inherent weakness of the old-fashioned corrupt deal was that, while it had powerful safeguards against exposure by its participants, it could not eliminate that danger completely. Occasionally, a party involved in a deal would reveal its terms to the public. Once one person talks, others tend to go public in hopes of minimizing damage to themselves, and the conspiracy falls apart.

The traditional response of the average citizen to exposure of government corruption was to recognize it as further evidence that government is inherently corrupt. *Of course* politicians steal and jobholders goldbrick; that's why government should be severely limited. What else is new? Political corruption was tolerated in the way that a shopkeeper tolerates petty shoplifting: it was wrong but inevitable. Just as the shopkeeper minimizes shoplifting by putting as little merchandise as possible where the shoplifter can grab it, so the citizen minimizes graft by putting as little money as possible in the public treasury where the politicians can grab it.

But in the aftermath of the outpouring of moral indignation that fueled the Civil War, Americans began to see politicians and government employees in a different light. No longer were politicians scoundrels distinguished from ordinary street criminals only by their gift of gab and their ability to wear civilized garb. Now politicians were moral leaders and government was a moral enterprise. The previous notion of law as suppressor of activities that were considered wrong by a broad consensus (e.g., murder, robbery, fraud) began to give way to the notion of law as positive agent for moral improvement (e.g., compulsory education, prohibition of alcohol, suppression of vice).

As people began to see government in this new way, their attitude toward corruption changed to one of moral outrage. No longer was corruption seen as an inevitable corollary of a necessary evil; now it was the result of evil people who had somehow managed to rise to positions of power and divert the state from its true purpose of improving humanity. These outbursts of public indignation gave rise to a reform movement for "civil service." The theory was simple: what enabled politicians to cheat the public was their authority to hire and fire government employees. Take away that authority, said the reformers, and the ranks of government employees would no longer be filled by people who depend on politicians for their livelihoods. Civil service reformers proposed to hire people on merit, as demonstrated by their ability to score well on civil service exams, and to promote them according to similar, seemingly-objective criteria; to prohibit civil servants from engaging in electoral politics (to prevent their constituting an electoral machine); and to prohibit or severely limit their ability to earn outside income (to prevent their using their jobs for personal gain). Civil service reform would attract a new kind of person to government employment — not political workers intent upon personal gain, but dedicated, selfless individuals dedicated to the public good.

As civil service gradually replaced the older "spoils" system, the political process changed in subtle ways. Politicians could no longer count on their job-holders to finance and provide manpower for their campaigns. They began to look to what are today called "special interests" to finance their campaigns and began to develop new and more subtle forms of profiting from their office.

Relieved of the need to make forced "contributions" to the campaign coffers and to beat the pavement on behalf of their bosses, government employment attracted a new sort of person. In some cases, I am sure, it attracted altruistic idealists determined to do good, as the reformers had promised. But it mostly attracted another sort: people who appreciated extremely secure jobs with very substantial benefit packages and relatively high pay, at which one need not work very hard.

For both the politician and the government employee, the method of converting public funds to personal funds had changed. But the opportunities and incentives to do so remained in place.

A dollar that is owned by the government is different from a dollar that is owned by an individual. When an individual hires someone, he requires that person to do his job, and to do it well and efficiently; he does not curry favors by hiring his friends' sexual partners or dim-witted brothers. When he buys a product, he makes sure that he gets it and it works; he does not buy $1,200 hammers or $25,000 toilet seats. When he makes an investment, he makes sure that it pays off; he does not lend money to the relatives of political friends so they can shore up the money-losing land-development venture in which they are partners with the governor. Failure to exercise diligence is tantamount to throwing away money.

When a politician or government employee hires someone, he is far less concerned with seeing that the person does his job well and efficiently. The cost of an incompetent or lazy employee comes not from his pocket, but from the taxpayer's. Before civil service reform, the politician or bureaucrat tended to hire individuals who were willing to kick back part of their wages, do personal favors, or show extraordinary political or personal loyalty. After civil service reform, the bureaucrat lost the power to select whom he hired. But he still had no particular incentive to see that an employee did his job efficiently. In fact, civil service reforms generally made it difficult or impossible to discharge an employee, unless the employee committed outright crimes or was grossly incompetent. So government bureaus were still filled with goldbrickers.

What's more, all but the lowest-level government employees still had certain discretion over the expenditure of tax money, with little incentive to seek efficiency or value. To prevent the old problem of kickbacks or favoritism, regulations were enacted, requiring competitive bids for larger contracts, review of contracts by superiors, and other safeguards. These regulations were inherently inefficient, but they seemed to reduce theft.

Politicians and bureaucrats have far less reason than businessmen to see that those they serve get what they pay for. What difference does it make to the bureaucrat whether he forces a remote underling to hire Gennifer Flowers or Roger Clinton instead of a competent person? Hiring a competent person makes the job of your underling easier; hiring Gennifer or Roger pleases someone with the power to advance your career or increase your agency's funding.

But politicians and bureaucrats have incentives to see that the money they control accrues benefits to themselves. Politicians no longer win elections by having party hacks take time off from government jobs to do petty favors for constituents, work the precincts, and get out the vote. Instead they hire campaign workers and buy advertising with funds provided by special interests. And if the special interests need to be paid off with a favorable contract, or regulation of a competitor, or protection from legitimate law enforcement, what's the problem? And if a little of that taxpayer money that pays back the donor finds its way into the politician's pocket, who's to care?

This widespread corruption is made possible by the virtual

absence in the process of anyone with an incentive to look out for the interests of the taxpayers. The politicians, the regulators, the attorneys, the bureaucrats, and the shady businessmen all benefit from the system and have no incentive to prevent waste. Literally everyone directly involved in the spending of government money is a beneficiary of that money; no one benefits from ensuring that it is spent efficiently or wisely. Is it any wonder that money finds its way into the pockets of those willing and able to work within the system?

The new class of bureaucrats and politicians solved the problem that had bedeviled the old class of party hacks and political bosses. Now, to avoid the danger of stool pigeonry by a participant in or witness to a corrupt deal, they simply never discuss terms or agree to any *quid pro quo.*

"Legal graft is the finder's fee, title insurance, city contracts," write Jack Newfield and Paul DuBrul in *The Abuse of Power.* "I'll get you a nursing home license and you give my friend some insurance." Members of the politico-bureaucratic class simply do favors for other members of their class, confident that those members will reciprocate. "It is important to understand," Newfield and DuBrul observe, "that above a certain level, there are no Democrats and no Republicans. . . . There are only class colleagues sharing profits."

And to discourage public revelation of these apparent but unprovable corrupt deals, they spread the money around. The taxpayer has infinitely deep pockets. By enabling the S&L crooks to use public funds as risk capital for speculative schemes, politicians in the 1980s didn't benefit only the wheeler-dealers. Yes, the bank officers and their confederates made millions, but some money found its way into the hands of politicians who took kickbacks, landowners whose land was purchased by the "developers" at inflated prices, investors who got over-market interest rates on government-guaranteed certificates of deposit, advertising copywriters for the promoters, and even (I suppose) tellers at the savings and loans.

With very few exceptions, even the press has little incentive to investigate these thefts of public money. For one thing, the attorneys who structure the deals are masters of misdirection and complication, making the task of investigation almost impossible. Furthermore, the pattern of corruption is so pervasive that the media have no rational criterion to select one particular episode for scrutiny. Unless, of course, the theft is particularly clumsy, or an especially high official is involved, as with Whitewater. (This is not to suggest that the media's lack of interest is uniform. Sometimes competition or partisan considerations breed good investigative journalism.)

So long as no explicit contracts are made, conspiracies against the public trust cannot be proven. Put nothing in writing, don't let anyone whose loyalty you have even the slightest doubt of know about the deal, and there's nothing anyone can prove.

Perhaps the first deal of this sort to become widely known came to light after Bess Myerson, the beauty queen turned game-show personality turned politician, was peripherally implicated in a political scandal in the administration of New York Mayor Ed Koch, then brought further attention to herself by being arrested for shoplifting. The resulting publicity stimulated interest in her past activities, eventually bringing a curious episode to light.

In the spring of 1983, Myerson was involved in a sexual relationship with Carl Andrew Capasso, a sewer contractor 20 years her junior who was in the midst of an angry divorce. Six days before a party in Myerson's honor at the mayor's mansion, Myerson added the name of Judge Hortense Gabel to the guest list and arranged to have a city car and chauffeur drive Mrs. Gabel to the party. A few days later, Myerson invited herself to a small dinner party at Gabel's house, and within a few weeks, Myerson was inviting Gabel to spend weekends at Capasso's estate in Westhampton. At some point, Judge Gabel introduced Myerson to her daughter, a well-educated young woman who had recently spent time in a psychiatric hospital.

Although the obese 39-year-old hadn't held a steady job in more than a decade, Myerson found her to have "extraordinary credentials" and a "brilliant resumé," which turned out to include such experiences as having "traveled alone, around the world" and "investigated the role of mentors in professional development." Myerson was in charge of the Cultural Affairs Department of New York City, a job she had received as a reward for campaigning on behalf of Mayor Ed Koch. Myerson was so impressed with the young woman that she appointed her to a high-paying job in her department.

Hortense Gabel was not just anybody. She was the judge who was presiding over the divorce of Myerson's young paramour. Although Judge Gabel was known as a "woman's judge," shortly after Myerson befriended her, she cut Andy Capasso's alimony in half. Judge Gabel was in the habit of having her law clerk write her decisions, but a few weeks after Myerson hired Gabel's otherwise unemployable daughter, she told her law clerk to turn over the Capasso file to her so she could write the decision herself. She cut Capasso's alimony by another third.

Virtually everyone in the political class in New York understood that the two events were not simply a coincidence, and the prosecutor went to court with virtually every conceivable piece of evidence except testimony or documentation of an explicit trade. There were dozens of witnesses to Myerson's favors done Judge Gabel. Myerson's staff testified at length that Gabel's daughter was hired under very strange circumstances for a job that she was not qualified to do. The judge's staff testified that Gabel handled the Capasso divorce far differently from her other cases; and, of course, her decision was substantially inconsistent with her past decisions in similar cases.

In the absence of proof of an explicit agreement, neither Myerson nor Judge Gabel nor Myerson's boyfriend was convicted of any wrongdoing. The case illustrated just how safe such corrupt transactions are from prosecution.

Myerson's case was archetypical of modern corruption as tacit *quid pro quo* in all respects but one: it came to public attention and was prosecuted. The facts emerged only after Myerson — a former television star, a megacelebrity, and the second most prominent politician in America's largest city — had been implicated in a scandal involving millions of dollars and the suicide of a prominent politician, and then got caught shoplifting. What are the chances that less blatant deals made by less prominent people will be exposed? Or deals by prominent people who have not humiliated themselves by being apprehended as petty criminals?

The pattern of institutional corruption is so widespread and the structures of the deals so complex that the press rarely gains much by exposure except in those very rare cases that involve very prominent people. Bess Myerson was one such case, and Bill and Hillary Clinton may be another.

Because they committed their theft of public funds in Arkansas, where old-style political corruption has never gone out of style and the risk of apprehension remains small, the Clintons appear to have structured their corrupt business the old-fashioned way — leaving a paper trail. Why else would the White House and the Rose Law Firm undertake such a massive destruction of evidence? Even with this fatal mistake, they would have gotten off scot-free, had Bill Clinton not been elected president, thereby attracting the interest of thousands of reporters lusting for a Pulitzer Prize.

After all, they only received a few tens of thousands of dollars and only cost the taxpayers a few tens of millions. This is pretty small stuff in a country where governments spend trillions of dollars each year.

Siphon-Off Economics

There is a curious parallel between the Clintons and the Huey Long administration of Louisiana. Like Huey Long, Bill Clinton focused his lust on power and showed little interest in money. Like Long's colleagues and heirs, Hillary Rodham Clinton wanted cash. She oversaw the family's finances, structured the corrupt deals, and apparently supervised the coverup. As their partner Diamond Jim McDougal told reporters, "If you tried to discuss finances or anything but politics with Bill, his eyes would glaze over. . . . Whatever we had to discuss, I discussed with her."

From the very start of their political life, she showed a weakness for money and a willingness to turn a blind eye toward conflicts of interest. Her admirers have made much of her meteoric "career" at the Rose Law Firm and as a director of various major corporations, ignoring the fact that she was hired by Rose only after her husband was elected attorney general and elevated to partner only after he was elected governor. In the corrupt atmosphere of Arkansas, it certainly didn't hurt Rose to have the attorney general's and then governor's wife on board. Indeed, it brought them substantial income, a small portion of which has come to the public's attention because of the Whitewater-Madison scandal. Nor did adding the governor's wife to the boards of directors of major Arkansas corporations do those companies any harm, especially when it became clear that the governor had a reasonable chance of one day becoming president.

And for much of the 1980s, Hillary Clinton had another motive to accumulate cash: her marriage was in serious trouble, and the possibility that it might end in divorce and financial insecurity had to be on her mind.

Whatever her motives, she behaved precisely like the greedy yuppies she and her husband publicly despised:

> For twelve years of this Reagan-Bush era, the Republicans have let S&L crooks and self-serving CEOs try to build an economy out of paper and perks instead of people and products. It's the Republican way: every man for himself and get it while you can. They stack the

deck in favor of their friends at the top and tell everybody else to wait for whatever trickles down. (Bill Clinton, campaign speech, November 20, 1991)

I was raised to believe the American dream was built on rewarding hard work. But we have seen the folks in Washington turn the American ethic on its head. For too long those who play by the rules and keep the faith have gotten the shaft. And those who cut corners and cut deals have been rewarded. (Bill Clinton, acceptance speech, July 16, 1992)

In addition to the corrupt political and business deals that have come to light in the past year, Hillary traded options and mutual funds and invested in sophisticated tax shelters. In one particularly interesting episode, she made a profit of $100,000 speculating in cattle futures.* By the time her husband was elected president, Hillary Rodham Clinton had accumulated nearly a million dollars.

Bill and Hillary share a lust for power, which they seem to enjoy both as an end in itself and as an instrument to other ends. Bill uses power to get sex, to impress a long line of small-town beauty queens and comely department-store clerks. Hillary uses power to get money, deftly trading her husband's influence for cold, hard cash, in the form of crooked deals with government contractors and other buyers of her husband's services.

As the public has gradually become aware of Hillary's

---

* Ms. Clinton claims that she was a typical commodity speculator, doing research by reading *The Wall Street Journal* and other public sources. It is a truism among futures traders that 95% of people who trade commodities lose their money and quit trading within a year. The tiny minority that is successful — and turning a small stake into $100,000 is wildly successful, by any standard — almost always continues to play commodities. But Hillary Clinton says that she took the $100,000 she made and walked away from the market never to play again. Given the close relationship of the Clintons to agribusinesses heavily involved in commodity trading, it is reasonable to surmise that the profit may have been a camouflaged bribe. An agribusiness can easily generate simultaneous losses and profits by going both long and short on the same commodity, then assigning the profitable trade to a favored trader (Ms. Clinton) and the losing trade to another (its house account).

responsibility for the Whitewater-Madison fraud, her reputation as a saint has wilted. The president has jumped to her defense, telling reporters that "I have never known a person with a stronger sense of right and wrong in my life — ever." This is a pretty tepid defense — Bill Clinton has focused his entire life on politics and associated almost exclusively with politicians, an occupation hardly characterized by powerful moral sense.

Of course, as the Whitewater scam has unraveled, Bill Clinton has become more and more involved. He has learned many of the details and worked to cover them up. But it is difficult even to imagine his concocting and executing the corrupt schemes that enriched his family, though he certainly did not object to them.

The Bottom Line

So long as government remains an ever-more-powerful institution, gobbling up people's money and restricting their freedom, corruption will grow and expand. For a century, most Americans have tried to pretend that the problem of corruption is the problem of a few bad people. They have ignored the fact that government attracts and rewards those who are already corrupt and presents corrupting incentives to those who are not.

Confronted with corruption, there is always a temptation to blame scandals entirely on their perpetrators — to say that they can be avoided by choosing better men and women to be our political leaders. This is a temptation that must be overcome if the corruption of our political culture is to be addressed.

Power tends to corrupt; absolute power corrupts absolutely. The only way to reduce corruption is to severely limit government's power to tax, spend, and regulate. Any other approach is bound to fail.

Was the Pet Removed from the Premises?

by Victor Niederhoffer and Caroline Baum

On October 11, 1978, a neophyte investor with a $25,000 annual income opened a commodity futures account with a deposit of $1,000. The first trade was the short sale of ten live cattle contracts at a price of 57.55 cents: a commitment to deliver in December of that year 400,000 pounds of cattle with a market value of $230,000.

One day later, the investor bought the contracts back at a price of 56.10 cents, just 0.15 cents above the low of the day, pocketing $5,300 for a return of 530%.

Except for her erroneous recollection that she reinvested the profits — she withdrew $5,000 from the account eleven days later — she does not remember any details of the trade. But 15 years later, when she took up residence in the White House, it became a matter of national interest.

Hilary (sic) Rodham, which is how her name appears on all of the Refco brokerage statements from the period, continued to be a net winner at the game. By the time she closed her trading account ten months later, she had racked up $99,537 in profits, a spectacular 10,000% return on her initial investment of $1,000. Either Ms. Rodham is the best trader to burst upon the scene since George Soros, whose 122% best-ever annual return in 30 years of trading pales by comparison, or else she was led by an invisible hand.

The first lady's detractors view her profits as an implicit bribe — a payment up front in return for a favor to be rendered once her husband became governor of Arkansas.

"It is inconceivable that the Clintons, who had virtually no money at the time, would even think of risking their limited resources in such a mad, highly leveraged gamble as trading cattle futures," wrote former racetrack handicapper and *New York Post* columnist Ray Kerrison. "Not, that is, unless somebody assured them beforehand of guaranteed profits."

Hillary started trading at the suggestion, and later with the advice, of family friend and Tyson Foods counsel James Blair in October 1978, one month before frontrunner Bill Clinton was elected governor of Arkansas. Tyson, the largest chicken processor in the world, was Arkansas' biggest employer. Chairman Don Tyson was part of an elite group of Arkansas businessmen who viewed their role in the political process as providing money and support for candidates who would be in a position to grant concessions and favors in the future.

Ms. Rodham and her supporters view things differently. Defending the legitimacy of her activities during her White House Dining Room press conference in April, the first lady attributed her success to Blair's "theory that because of the economy in the early part of the 1970s, a lot of cattle herds had been liquidated, so that there was going to be a big opportunity to make money in the late '70s."

After examining Hillary's trading records, both Leo Melamed, the father of financial futures and former chairman of the Chicago Mercantile Exchange, and Jack Sandner, the Merc's current chairman, found nothing irregular except, on occasion, insufficient margin in her account. Anyone could have done as well, these respected gentlemen said, given the doubling of cattle prices during her year of trading.

Mr. Melamed called the brouhaha over the first lady's financial affairs "a tempest in a teapot." Mr. Sandner wrote off her success to her "trading the biggest bull market in the history of cattle. If someone caught that trend and traded it well, they could make an extraordinary amount of money, a lot more than $100,000 on a small investment."

Ms. Rodham *bucked* the trend and traded it well. Eleven of her 20 cattle trades were initiated from the short side. Short-selling by the public is extremely rare, especially on a first trade. When one considers that both the investor and her trading advisor were using a herd-reduction theory to capitalize on the biggest bull market in cattle in history, the success of her short sales raises a bright red flag.

In a bestselling book on cattle trading in the '90s, George Horace Lorimar made some timeless observations concerning the relationship between the return and the legitimacy of any investment:

> You must learn not to overwork a dollar anymore than you would a horse. Three percent is a small load for it to draw; six a safe one; when it makes twenty you own a blame good critter or a mighty foolish one, and you want to make dead sure which; but if it draws a hundred it's playing the races or something just as hard on horses and dollars, and the first thing you know you won't have even a carcass to haul to the glue factory.

That those observations were made about the 1890s in no way mitigates the message. Ms. Rodham's 10,000% return stands out as overwork by any yardstick in any year.

In other situations where a transaction's legitimacy is suspect, the courts are guided by the common law doctrine, recently enunciated by Supreme Court Justice Scalia, that "a transfer of title for a grossly inadequate (or in some cases grossly excessive) consideration would raise a rebuttable presumption of actual fraudulent intent" (*BFP v. Resolution Trust Corporation*, 62 U.S.L.W. 4359, U.S. Supreme Court, decided May 23, 1994).

The first lady's pretty-in-pink press conference in April of 1994 was designed to rebut the presumption of fraudulent intent, but it failed to exonerate her from the suspicion that something was amiss in her financial dealings of the later 1970s.

Traces of Fraud

Cases of fraud are notoriously hard to prove; most perpetrators use great ingenuity in disguising their acts. In the investigation of a suspected fraud, the prosecutor does not expect to uncover a document outlining the terms of an illicit financial transfer between two parties. Similarly, an insurance investigator does not expect to find an arsonist standing on the fire-ravaged premises with match and empty gasoline can in hand.

But the clues are there, waiting to be uncovered. Often a minor deception trips a switch, exposing layers of inconsistencies and forcing the perpetrator to spin an ever-more intricate web, which ultimately traps him in what was supposed to be a defensive net.

It is said that there is no such thing as a perfect crime, only an imperfect investigation. Despite their best efforts, perpetrators of fraud usually leave a slimy trail — what fraud investigators refer to as badges or indicia.

> Fraud has to be ferreted out by carefully following its marks and signs, for fraud will in most instances, though never so artfully and secretly contrived, like the snail in its passage, leave its slime by which it may be traced. (*Floyd v. Goodwin*, 16 Tenn., 484, 490: 1835)

Insurance investigators have an objective list of marks and signs that they look for when a presumption of fraud exists. For example, in cases where arson is suspected, one of the first questions a fire investigator tries to answer is: Was the pet removed from the premises? Medical fraud might be indicated in cases where the medical bills in question are photocopies, or if they fail to itemize office visits and treatments. In cases of automobile accident fraud, one marker would be a claimant's attempt to discourage an insurance investigator from looking at the damaged vehicle.

As far as we know, there are no indicia for commodities trading fraud. So we took it upon ourselves to develop a checklist of fraud indicators that would be applicable to a broad range of financial trickery. Doubtless the reader could add to or amend our list. But we are confident that any investment activity that scores high on our test merits a red flag of malfeasance. We have used ten criteria to rate the likely legitimacy of Ms. Rodham's activities on a scale ranging from one (highly likely) to ten (100-to-1 odds against).

(1) *Were the returns excessive as measured against a normal yardstick of performance?* Yes. As discussed above, Ms. Rodham's annual return was more than 80 times George Soros' in his best year. As far as we know, no non-professional has ever achieved a return of that magnitude. Stanley Kroll, a well-known commodities broker who worked at three major firms at the time of Hillary's trades, has written that none of his retail customers turned a profit. Neither did those of any of his colleagues at other firms. Even Ms. Rodham's trading advisor, Jim Blair, who by his own admission was "damn good" at making money in commodities, declared bankruptcy with a $15 million trading loss shortly after his pupil stopped trading herself. Score: ten points.

(2) *Has there been any effort to suppress investigation of the transaction?* Yes. Ms. Rodham was adamantly opposed to the appointment of a special prosecutor to look into the Clinton's financial dealings, including her own trading activities, during the late 1970s and 1980s. What's more, she attempted to deflect attention from the matter by explaining away the source of her new-found wealth as a gift from her parents until the Clintons' 1978 and 1979 tax returns were made public and the actual source of her windfall profit was revealed. Score: ten points.

(3) *Are crucial records of the transaction missing or available only in duplicate form?* Yes. The purchase and sale confirmations for Ms. Rodham's two most profitable trades are lost or missing. Her first, extraordinary transaction is also listed among the missing. The details were furnished by the Chicago Mercantile Exchange. Backup is available for 30 of the 33 total transactions.

Ms. Rodham has no independent recollection of her first

trade, which produced a 530% return overnight. You can be sure that Fernando Valenzuela hasn't forgotten the five shutouts in his first seven games as a rookie pitcher for the Los Angeles Dodgers in 1981. Score: ten points.

(4) *Did the suspect alter her story regarding the activity in question?* Yes. The White House furnished ever-changing versions of Ms. Rodham's trading activities. First they said she did all of her own research, relying primarily on *The Wall Street Journal,* and placed all of her own trades. Then they said mentor James Blair played an advisory role, but she made the decisions, determined the size, and placed all of the trades. As the story now stands, she relied on Blair's advice, and he placed most of her trades.

When queried, the first lady explained that the confusion was the result of the way the story was communicated to the press. Score: ten points.

(5) *Was a good portion of the purchases and sales executed near the most favorable prices of the day?* Yes. Hillary's first trade of 10 live cattle contracts (sold short) was entered on October 11, 1978 and covered 24 hours later. Her respective entry and exit prices were 57.55 and 56.10. The low on October 12 was 55.95. The chances of a retail trader buying at a price 15 ticks off the intraday low on a ten-contract trade are about as good as those of finding the Dead Sea Scrolls on the steps of the State House in Little Rock.

Many of her subsequent transactions were executed near the day's extremes, including her last big trade in July 1979. At a time when her account was $18,000 underwater, she managed to sell 50 live cattle contracts 0.12 cents from the high on a day when prices dropped the $1.50 limit. Her very last trade was a purchase of 50 cattle contracts just 0.05 cents above the low of the day. Such precision trading is enviable for any on- or off-floor trader who spends every second of the trading day glued to the screen. It is a dazzling coup for a non-professional like Ms.

Rodham, who had many other claims on her time, such as litigating for Rose, serving on corporate boards, crusading for children's rights, serving as chairman of the Legal Services Corporation, and performing various duties as the governor's wife.

Until Hillary's diaries and Rose's time sheets become a matter of public record and reveal her whereabouts between 10:05 a.m. and 2:00 p.m. Eastern Standard Time, Monday through Friday, we cannot award her a perfect score. Score: eight points.

(6) *Was there anything unusual about the suspect's behavior or anything irregular about the activity in question?* Yes. As mentioned earlier, Ms. Rodham, a neophyte investor with nearly no savings, traded the biggest bull market in the history of cattle primarily from the short side. Her first three transactions were short sales.

The irregularities connected with her first trade alone should have tripped the security system. The commission of $500 and bid-asked spread of around $600 on such a trade came to more than her entire initial equity of $1,000, which was all she wished to put at risk. So from the moment she entered her first transaction she had already lost more than she could afford to lose.

Unlike that of most traders, Hillary's trading activity reveals no discernible pattern. She bought and sold everything from one and two lots to 60 contracts at a time. In her waning days as a speculator, she day-traded 50 contracts at a time when she already had an open position of 65 contracts. Score: ten-plus points.

(7) *Was the risk on the trade inconsistent with the customer's net income and net worth?* Yes. Ms. Rodham's 1978 earned income of $24,250 from her Rose Law Firm partnership and husband Bill's $26,500 as Arkansas attorney general are considerably lower than the minimums set by most brokerage houses for opening a commodities trading account. If for some reason Ms. Rodham had lost rather than won $100,000, where would she

have come up with the money?

On three separate occasions (in November 1978, December 1978, and July 1979), the value of Ms. Rodham's open positions was well in excess of $1 million for days at a time, and in two cases for up to three weeks. A 2% to 5% move — a move that occurs about once every two weeks — in the wrong direction would have wiped out not only their net income for the year but also their entire net worth. The Clintons' joint political aspirations would have gone up in smoke if the governor-elect had been forced to declare personal bankruptcy as a result of his wife's speculations in the risky world of commodities futures. Score: ten points.

(8) *Was the suspect in a position to do a favor for any of the other parties involved?* Yes. Hillary got involved in commodity trading at the suggestion of Tyson Foods counsel Jim Blair, who subsequently advised her on all of her trades. Tyson Foods Chairman Don Tyson viewed "politics as a series of unsentimental transactions between those who need votes and those who have money . . . a world where every quid has its quo" (*New York Times Magazine*, July 31, 1994).

Clearly Tyson had money, and he put it on Bill Clinton in 1978. In return, as reported in the *New York Times Magazine*, he expected the new governor to raise the legal truck weight limit in Arkansas so that Tyson Foods could compete with out-of-state poultry truckers.

Blair, in addition to his ties with Tyson, may have been balancing an item in his own account. Prior to Ms. Rodham's trading, in the early months of the Carter administration, Clinton coordinated federal patronage in Arkansas, and one of his first moves in this area was to recommend Blair for the chairmanship of the Federal Home Loan Bank Board.

In his book *Keys to Crookdom*, written in 1924, George C. Henderson comments: "The great grafter does not buy government officials after they are elected, as a rule. He owns them beforehand." And, in a hauntingly prescient conclusion: "Occasionally good and faithful servants are rewarded by attorney's fat fees, gifts and market tips in addition to emoluments of the office." Score: ten points.

(9) *Was there any history of illegal, irregular, or unethical behavior on the part of the broker?* Yes. Red Bone, the broker of record for both Mr. Blair and Ms. Rodham, was suspended from trading for a year even before he left Tyson Foods to run the Springdale Refco office, for trying to corner the egg futures market. In 1979, Red was disciplined by the CME for "serious and repeated violations of record-keeping functions, order-entry procedures, margin requirements and hedge procedures." Refco was fined $250,000, which at the time was the largest fine ever levied for commodity-trading violations.

One of Refco's Springdale brokers at the time has admitted under oath that the firm was buying and selling blocks of contracts and allocating them to customers after the market closed. In one instance, after being chastised by their superiors in Refco's Chicago headquarters, the brokers had to set back the time stamp clock and engage in a marathon session of back-clocking all of the day's trades in order to give the appearance that account allocations had been properly made. Score: ten points.

(10) *Were rules, regulations, and normal operating procedures violated?* Yes. Ms. Rodham insists that despite the advice she received from James Blair, she maintained a non-discretionary account. Any non-broker who places an order for a customer is, by definition, acting in a discretionary capacity and must file the appropriate documents. Furthermore, in view of Ms. Rodham's busy schedule and the precision timing of many of her trades, it is likely that Blair placed the orders without consulting her. It would appear that a host of rules and regulations was violated.

Finally, it is inconceivable that a prudent broker would

assume all of the risk exposure for a client who did not have the funds to support her positions without a third-party guarantee. Score: ten points.

Total Score: 98

A Closer Look

According to our profile, Hillary scored 98 out of a possible 100 on our financial hanky-panky scale, catapulting her to the top of the class for potential commodities fraud. A score of ten on any of the criteria corresponds to a chance of legitimacy of 1 in 100. Assuming each score is independent, the chances of legitimacy of Hillary's trades is approximately one in two hundred quadrillion.

A detailed examination of Ms. Rodham's trades seemed in order. We started with records of each purchase and sale confirmation, and all of the monthly statements that were provided by the White House. Next we looked at the high, low, open, and close on each of these days to see how her fills compared to what was available. Finally, we calculated the unrealized gains, required margin, available equity, and commitments outstanding for each day during Ms. Rodham's ten months of trading. Inspired by the legendary trackers of the past, and armed with legions of data, we were prepared to rebut the first lady's contention that "there isn't any evidence that anybody gave me any favorable treatment."

Our analysis of the data and other documents yielded the following observations:

(1) Ms. Rodham's account was under-margined by $50,000 to $80,000 during a one-month period beginning November 10, 1978. Again, in July 1979, her margin requirements were approximately $100,000 for several days, when there was negative equity (minus $30,000) in the account. A normal rule of thumb for commodity traders is to maintain equity of at least five times the margin requirement. Ms. Rodham routinely

reversed this ratio, maintaining equity of around one-fifth of her required margin.

(2) Her total equity would have been wiped out on three occasions, taking into account the commissions due and the cost of exiting the trades. On July 17, the commissions and bid-asked spreads on newly opened positions, added to her existing deficit going into the day, could have been enough to totally wipe out the entire family's net worth, even without any market move against her.

(3) Her name was misspelled ("Hilary") on all of the official brokerage statements she produced, raising the question of whether or not the statements were ever mailed to the detail-oriented attorney.

(4) Her first two monthly statements reveal identical misalignments and faulty keystrokes on certain letters, raising doubts as to their authenticity. It wouldn't take a great stretch of the imagination to conclude that they were generated simultaneously in an effort to cover the slimy trail.

(5) Withdrawals from her account consistently kept her equity below $15,000. After each big win, she withdrew the spoils. Finally, after making about $100,000 in four days in July 1979, she closed her account down. Such behavior is inconsistent with human nature, as observed any day in Las Vegas or Atlantic City, as well as Ms. Rodham's claim that she reinvested her profits.

(6) Two-thirds of her trades showed a profit by the close of the day she entered them, and 80% of her trades, on both the long and the short sides, were ultimately profitable, percentages that are rarely achieved by the most successful professionals.

(7) Commissions and slippage on her trades totaled more than 37 times her initial equity, yet she still managed to net more than a 10,000% return.

(8) Most of her 33 trades were for five or ten lots. But on three occasions, Ms. Rodham traded 50 or 60 contracts: posi-

tions that would normally require around $1 million in equity to support. Each of these three trades was entered at extraordinarily favorable levels relative to the price range of the day, and was highly profitable by day's end. On two of the large trades, the overnight profits pushed a negative existing equity into the black. Had she lost on any of these large trades, the implications for her "investment program" would have been dire.

(9) For a two-week period in July 1979, the equity in her account swung from negative $31,000 to positive $62,000. Finally, after buying 50 contracts just a gnat's eyelash above the low of the day, the account was closed with a withdrawal of $60,000, making total withdrawals of over $99,000. Ms. Rodham was allowed to trade like a millionaire in order to bring her equity out of the red and into the black, in the process violating numerous rules and procedures that industry professionals have developed to prevent financial catastrophe to customer and brokerage house alike.

More egregious than any of the previous red flags of commodities trading fraud was the size of Ms. Rodham's commitments. From day one, the size of her positions was wildly out of line with the equity available to absorb loss. On November 13, 1978, with $13,000 in her account, she controlled a position of 62 contracts with an underlying market value of $1.9 million. On December 11, 1978, Ms. Rodham had $6,000 in her account and a 90-contract position valued at $2.3 million. And on her third-to-last day of trading, July 17, 1979, she had 115 contracts outstanding with a market value of $3.2 million. The equity in her account was a negative $18,000.

The daily fluctuations in the price of Hillary's cattle commitments taken in 1978 and 1979 averaged 1% a day from close to close and 2% from high to low. On unusual days, once or twice a month, cattle prices fluctuate 4% or 5%. All commodity traders know that they must be sufficiently liquid to withstand such extreme swings and avoid financial ruin.

One 4% or 5% adverse fluctuation in Ms. Rodham's position would have constituted five times her annual income and five times her net worth. And this is just a one-day move. Commodities have a nasty habit of moving against you several days in a row, right to the point that you are forced to liquidate.

But not Ms. Rodham. Whenever she was on the brink of ruin, she managed to pull a rabbit out of a hat.

The outlook was not bright for Ms. Rodham in the middle of July 1979. The total equity in her account was a negative $31,245. She owed $65,000 in margin requirement. On July 17, she doubled up, selling 50 more contracts just 0.12 cents off the day's high of 68.72, and covering it that same day for a profit of $10,400. At the time that Hillary entered the trade, her required margin was $115,000 and her total cash due to the broker was $135,000. Imagine what would have happened if cattle had closed limit up that day, instead of limit down.

Such huge bets in the clinch are reminiscent of the legendary Oriental gambler who, after having wagered away his last cent, stakes the personal liberty of his wife, children, and even himself on a final roll of the dice.

Most American speculators know, however, that doubling up when one's position is seriously underwater is a one-way ticket to ruin. Only if she had held a confirmed, round-trip ticket would someone in Ms. Rodham's position have been willing to risk the farm in such a high-stakes game.

Providentially, three days later, on her last day of trading, the whole situation was resolved. Cattle closed limit down again and Ms. Rodham covered her short position just 0.05 cents above limit down.

Ms. Rodham ended her career as a speculator with a final flourish to rival her first trade. She never traded through Refco again.

After extensive research into Ms. Rodham's trading activities of 15 years ago, we have satisfied ourselves that Ms. Rodham was neither naive nor lucky nor particularly talented as a trader. She was, however, gracious in accepting a gift from those in a position to benefit once her husband became governor of Arkansas. Even individuals who have never visited a futures exchange or traded one futures contract will, upon examination of the evidence, be convinced that Ms. Rodham's activity at the time and her representation of the events 15 years later are highly implausible.

After mobilizing our combined resources and knowledge, after hours of exhaustive study and research, after a concerted attempt to follow the path and uncover the truth, we are still left with one gnawing question. Ms. Rodham earned profits of $99,537. What happened to the other $463?

The Great Bimbo Eruption of '93

by Chester Alan Arthur

When I first heard that several Arkansas state troopers who had provided security service to Bill Clinton were revealing details about Clinton's sex life — private life would be a misnomer these days — I figured there wouldn't be much we could learn about our president from them. After all, revelations that emerged during the presidential campaign pretty much established that Clinton had the opportunity, appetite, and inclination for extramarital sex, and a willingness to deceive women attracted to his position of power and/or personal charm. We further knew that he had violated public ethics (and the law) by rewarding at least one of his sex partners with a government job. All the new reports could do is add a few colorful details to what we already knew.

The story broke on Sunday, December 20, when CNN reported that *The American Spectator*, a conservative monthly, was about to publish an article by David Brock which reported the allegations of the state troopers. The *Spectator* article appeared the next day; the day after that, The *Los Angeles Times* published a front-page article detailing its own investigation of the same story.

Brock's account in the *Spectator* is a breezily written summary of the background to the story and a narrative of the troopers' revelations, with a fair amount of colorful detail and an unmistakable hostility to Clinton. My first reaction was to object to its lead paragraph, a summary of an August 1992 *Washington Post* report about a Clinton aide's efforts to control what she called "bimbo eruptions." What was strange was Brock's characterization of the report as "little noticed" — I had heard it more than once, and I am not a reader of the *Post*.

The article mostly filled in details, as I had anticipated. There were some revelations, but most were not very surprising. The troopers reported that Clinton habitually had sex with a rather large number of women, which I hadn't known before — but I wasn't surprised. The troopers reported that Clinton was often unpleasant and inconsiderate to them, but no man is a hero to his valet. Nor was I astonished at his temper tantrums, his "outsized ego," or the fact that he is "personable" — these are very commonly characteristics of successful politicians. Even the report that Clinton continued to have illicit sex after his election didn't really surprise me: old habits are hard to break.

The troopers also reported that they did a lot of personal errands for him, including arranging meetings with women to whom Clinton had taken a shine, guarding his privacy during his assignations, and helping him deceive Hillary about the extent of his adultery. I am not as upset by this as the *Spectator* hoped I would be — it seems to me that in our society using security forces as servants is generally considered to be one of the perks of high political office. Yes, there were some small but interesting details: Clinton's worrying about whether he could possibly earn a living if he were unable to continue his career as a politician, his ruminations about his personal stardom, his gargantuan appetites, his being briefed on the price of various common grocery items so he could avoid the sort of embarrassment Bush suffered when he appeared unable to recognize a supermarket scanner. ("When Clinton was later asked by a viewer on CBS *This Morning* if he knew the price of bread and milk, and he answered correctly, campaign strategist James Carville cited this performance in a *New York Times* op-ed piece as an example of Clinton's ability 'to empathize with average people.'")

The troopers' reports about Hillary's extramarital sexual activities did have some significance. Of course, I wasn't surprised by the fact of her adultery — after all, it has been plain for some time that she and Bill were probably not having sexual relations. But the troopers substantiated a rumor that has been making the rounds for over a year: that she and Vincent Foster had a long-term affair prior to his suicide. This is significant — if corroborated — because of the unusual circumstances surrounding Foster's suicide: the fact that Clinton aides searched his office and removed various papers, while keeping police investigators away; his delphic suicide note, which seemed to suggest he was uncomfortable testifying about the Clintons' investments in Whitewater Development and the related failure of an Arkansas savings and loan, bailed out by the taxpayers to the tune of $47 million.

The *Los Angeles Times* piece was a straight news report. In contrast to Brock's story, it was objective journalism of a very high order. *Times* reporters William C. Rempel and Douglas Frantz attempted to corroborate as much of the troopers' revelations as they could. They found, for example, telephone records that indicated that Clinton made extensive phone calls to some of the women with whom the troopers alleged he had sexual relations, including a 94-minute call placed at 1:23 a.m., followed by an 18-minute call at 7:45. They also contacted the women whose names were revealed, all of whom either denied a sexual relationship or refused to speak at all. They also verified details with other state troopers, who refused to sign affidavits or make their names published, and investigated the backgrounds and reputations of the troopers involved.

The first media analysis I saw of the troopers' revelations came only two days after the story broke, when *Nightline* devoted a half hour to the story. For me the highlight of the program was the following analysis from Sidney Blumenthal, political editor of *The New Yorker*:

> This strikes me as a large, deliberate distraction. I think that what we do know is that there is a small, far right-wing group of people, who through these disgruntled state troopers have put out uncorroborated, salacious details and through that have been able to pull the

strings of the mainstream media and sending them I think like mindless gumshoes down blind alleys. To the extent that there has been some independent inquiry into this, what we have found, for the most part, are refutations of these charges. Now I wish to add that not only is Cliff Jackson involved whom you mentioned in your earlier report who has been engaged in a very long time personal and political vendetta against the president, but a younger right-wing writer — I hesitate to call him a journalist — David Brock, who has written on Anita Hill and accused her of being part of a conspiracy and a perjurer, charges that were very convincingly refuted in *The New Yorker*, my magazine, by two *Wall Street Journal* writers. Now in his report, he produces charges made by these troopers about the first lady's so-called sexual activities. They're quite lurid, they're quite explicit, about her affairs. Now either they're true or they're not true. Now Brock has said in The *Washington Post* of tomorrow that will appear tomorrow that the evidence is purely circumstantial. In other words, more uncorroborated evidence. Well either it's all true or it's not.

This is a remarkable reaction. Instead of responding to a single bit of evidence, Blumenthal launched a personal attack on Brock and *The American Spectator*, blaming the whole affair on the "far right wing." Apparently he hadn't noticed that the story was first investigated by the *Times*, which spent over four months investigating it, and published substantially the same findings as the *Spectator*. He concludes his case against the charges by observing that Brock not only reported what the troopers had told him about Clinton's extramarital recreation, but also about the extramarital activities of his wife, and pointing out that Brock's story is "either all true or it's not." He doesn't mention the possibility that it might be partly true or mostly true, nor that Brock was not accusing the first lady, but merely reporting the statements of witnesses who claimed to have first-hand evidence of her adultery.

His only comment on the evidence is that it is "uncorroborated" and "circumstantial." There are three kinds of evidence: confession, the statements of witnesses, and physical (i.e., circumstantial). Two witnesses have made public statements and two others have made statements privately to reporters. In addition, three Arkansas women have publicly stated that they were sexual partners with Clinton. In addition, reporters for both the *Los Angeles Times* and the *Spectator* discovered substantial corroborating physical evidence. If Bill Clinton were on trial for adultery, this would be ample evidence to convince a jury of Clinton's guilt.

But it fails to make the slightest impression on Blumenthal. The testimony of four witnesses and three participants he dismisses as "uncorroborated." The physical evidence he dismisses as "circumstantial." What is Blumenthal waiting for? A photograph of Clinton and a non-Hillary woman in *flagrante delicto*? A notarized confession from Clinton himself?

Whether David Brock is a journalist is not plain, but it is certain that Sidney Blumenthal is not. Characterizing Sidney Blumenthal as an apologist or as a public relations flack may even be too generous.

Meanwhile, *The New Republic's* Michael Kinsley led his commentary on the piece with the same observation I had made. "*Little noticed?*" Kinsley italicizes. "The implication is that Brock has picked up some important but overlooked piece of evidence here." Indeed, Kinsley had done a search of the Nexis database of "newspapers, magazines, wire services, and television transcripts" and noted that the "bimbo eruption" locution had appeared some 324 times.

He then accused Brock of inaccurately characterizing in the second paragraph of his *Spectator* piece the article from the *Post* in which the phrase had appeared. "Anyway, those are the first two paragraphs of Brock's piece," Kinsley writes. "You can judge the next 120 or so paragraphs on that basis."

I was stunned. Kinsley expects us to judge "120 or so" paragraphs on the basis of his relatively minor quibbles with the first two? No, not exactly. "These minor matters don't prove the untruth of Brock's major accusations. But they do prove his fundamental bad faith, and that of his editors."

Well, I'm not sure what "bad faith" constitutes in this context. If Kinsley means that neither Brock nor his editors support Clinton, then he is surely correct. If he means that Brock intentionally lied about Clinton . . . well, here his case is weak. If he means that Brock is a sloppy journalist who is letting his evaluation of Clinton overshadow his judgment, and that his editors are not performing their proper critical role . . . well, he might be right. But maybe he should focus the same critical eye on his own writing.

Aside from criticisms of Brock's first two paragraphs, Kinsley pretty much limits himself to quoting a few items from the trooper's statements and saying that he finds them unbelievable. With one exception, Kinsley offers no evidence.

One of the troopers told Brock that Clinton was angry at Dukakis for making Clinton look like a fool at the 1988 convention, and that as a result, according to the trooper, Clinton "refused to endorse him [Dukakis] until a few weeks before the election." Kinsley reports he did another search of the Nexis database and came up with a "whole string" of endorsements of Dukakis by Clinton, and concludes the trooper is "unreliable."

He does not consider the possibility that the trooper's statement about Clinton's belated endorsement of Dukakis may have been based on the trooper's observations of Clinton's private hostility, or that the trooper didn't read any of the newspapers, magazines, and television transcripts in the Nexis database in which Kinsley had found the "whole string" of endorsements. Or that the trooper simply had a lapse of memory which might not render everything else he and the other trooper said "patently unreliable." Put yourself in the place of the trooper, whose job required him to serve Clinton at every task from providing security to cleaning up after Socks the cat. Would you be more likely to remember the events of a political campaign five years ago, or whether you had seen Clinton receive a blow job from a department store clerk in a car in Chelsea's elementary school parking lot while you kept other cars away?

Kinsley follows this up with three statements from the troopers about Clinton's private behavior that Kinsley does not believe, though Kinsley offers no evidence to the contrary. Here is Kinsley's summary and criticism of one paragraph from Brock's article:

> Do you believe that the Clintons "wouldn't go out to dinner with friends the way you or I would"? Too snobbish, according to one of Brock's troopers. Bob Woodward could probably nail this one down. Pending that, though, is this plausible?

Here is the paragraph from Brock's article:

> Hillary, as described by the troopers, pursued power with a single-minded intensity, had few friends outside politics, and was not especially close to her family. "Everything was politics. They wouldn't go out to dinner with friends the way you or I would or the way I've seen [the current Arkansas governor] do," said Perry. "If they were invited to a private party, and there were only going to be eight or ten people there, she could say, 'We're not going to waste time at that thing. There aren't enough people there.' I never saw Hillary just relax and have a good time."

At no point does Brock (or one of the troopers) suggest that the Clintons didn't enjoy a normal social life because they were "too snobbish." Kinsley is guilty of mischaracterization, the same offense he believes is sufficient basis to "prove a fundamental bad faith" by Brock and Brock's editors.

To sum up, from a 13-page article consisting mostly of statements by troopers assigned to provide security for Clinton during a 13-year period, Kinsley cites one allegation from one trooper that is false and three that he does not believe, and concludes that the troopers are "patently unreliable." Like Blumenthal, he has made himself an apologist for Clinton. This is a very sad development. Kinsley is an intelligent man and a fine writer. He has no reason to prostitute himself.

Mass Murder, American Style

by R.W. Bradford

Janet Reno, the nation's top law enforcement agent, is a mass murderer. We know this because she confessed to it on national television on April 19, 1993.

On April 18, by her own statement, she ordered the FBI to take what it characterized as "the next logical step in a series of actions to bring this episode [the standoff between the FBI and the Branch Davidian community] to a conclusion." That "logical step" was to send a Bradley M-728s "combat engineering vehicles" (tanks) to punch holes in the walls of the buildings in which the Davidians lived, and to pump poisonous tear gas into their homes at 15 second intervals, while FBI loudspeakers proclaimed, "This is not an assault."

"I made the decision," Reno told reporters that afternoon. "I'm accountable. The buck stops with me and nobody ever accused me of running from a decision that I made based on the best information that I had. The buck stops with me."

That evening, in an interview with Ted Koppel, she elaborated:

> This was a judgment I made. I investigated it completely. I did all the — I asked the questions, I talked to the experts when I had questions, and I think the responsibility lies with me . . . I made the best judgment I could based on all the information that we had after inquiry, after talking with experts, after trying to weigh all the terrible possibilities that could take place now or later. I've made the judgment, it's my judgment, I stand by it.

What information did Ms. Reno get from the experts in her Federal Bureau of Investigation? According to statements from the FBI and from Ms. Reno, the FBI believed the following:

(1) That David Koresh, leader of the Branch Davidians, had

been placed under serious stress by the events of the previous seven weeks. He had been shot during the armed confrontation of February 28 and his infant daughter had been killed. He was in a terrible situation, his home surrounded by heavily armed men intent on capturing or killing him and destroying the religious community he headed.

(2) That the stress on Koresh had gotten worse during the standoff, thanks to the tactics of the FBI, which had blasted him and his community with ear-shattering noise, aimed powerful electric spotlights into their windows at night to prevent them from sleeping, turned off their water supply, and cut off their sewers. Apparently, the intent was to drive Koresh crazy — to "ratchet up the pressure," in the words of FBI spokesman Bob Ricks.

(3) That Koresh had publicly said that in the event of a confrontation, the standoff would "end with people devoured by fire."

(4) That the Davidians were likely to attempt mass suicide if confronted. Even President Clinton was informed in advance of this risk, if we are to believe what he said at his informal press conference the next morning. He said they chose the tank-and-gas assault as "the best way to get people out of the compound quickly before they could kill themselves."

(5) That the wooden buildings in the compound, filled with baled hay, flammable liquids, and explosive and incendiary ammunition, were a terrible fire hazard, especially once the FBI punched huge holes in their walls through which wind could blow and spread any fire quickly.

(6) That there were 30-mile-per-hour winds in the area on the day of the assault. These would spread any fire very quickly.

It is not difficult to predict the effect of the "logical next step" of an assault on the compound: if several hours of tanks firing poisonous gas into the compound did not ignite the structures, the ammunition, or the fuel stored there, then the unstable leader of the Davidians, made more unstable by the FBI's "psychological" campaign to deny him sleep or peace or quiet, who had predicted the standoff would end with "people devoured by fire" and perhaps discussed and even planned a "mass suicide" in the event of an assault, would ignite the place himself. Given the high winds, the flammability of the buildings, the buildings' incendiary and explosive contents, and the fact that the FBI had cut off water to the area but not brought in fire-fighting equipment, Reno's decision made the deaths of the nearly 100 people a virtual certainty.

By her own admission, Janet Reno had "asked the questions and investigated it completely," so she knew all this. She had weighed "all the terrible possibilities that could take place," including the virtual certainty that the Davidians — including the dozens of children present — would be burned to death.

Knowing all this, she ordered the assault. "I've made the judgment," Janet Reno said. "It's my judgment. I stand by it. The responsibility lies with me." The assault she ordered could only end with the deaths of nearly 100 people, including a substantial number of people she knew to be innocent.

There is a term for what Janet Reno did. That term is mass murder.

There is one other possibility: that Reno was lying when she uttered those words. Successful politicians are characterized by adaptability, adeptness at misrepresenting situations and motives, and a skill at manipulating public opinion. It is entirely possible that Reno paid little attention to the Waco situation because she was preoccupied with political problems in Washington, that she uncritically accepted the FBI's plan of action, and that she developed the explanation for her actions — the explanation that amounted to a confession of mass murder — only as a public relations ploy, after the disaster had occurred.

If this is the case, then Reno is innocent of mass murder, the crime to which she confessed. She would instead be guilty of mass negligent homicide — a lesser crime, perhaps, but a serious crime nonetheless.

Janet Reno and the FBI offered excuses for their action. The assault, they claimed, was intended "to increase the pressure to bring about serious negotiations." But early that morning, the FBI told neighbors "that it would end today," and telephoned the compound, "At this point, we're not negotiating. We say, come on out, come out with your hands up. This matter is over."

Janet Reno told Ted Koppel the night of the assault that she had ordered the assault in order to protect the children from abuse. President Clinton backed up her claim at his press conference: "I talked to her [Janet Reno] on Sunday, I said, now, I want you to tell me once more why *you* believe, not why *they* believe, why *you* believe, we should move now rather than wait some more. And she said it's because of the children — they have evidence that those children are still being abused and that they're in increasingly unsafe conditions and that they don't think it will get any easier with time, with the passage of time."

But when Ted Koppel confronted her with testimony from a witness who had been in the compound and seen no signs of abuse (and who had reported the same to the FBI), Janet Reno admitted that they had no recent evidence of abuse. But, she added, "The sanitation situation within the compound we were told was beginning to deteriorate."

This theme was reiterated by Bill Clinton ("the children . . . being forced to live in unsanitary and unsafe conditions") and FBI spokesman Jeff Jamar, who told reporters, "How would the federal government look, when we finally get in the compound, there are children dying of hunger or children dying of disease because of the conditions? That was one of the overriding concerns." So the abuse that the FBI and attorney general accuse the Davidians of consisted of denying them proper food, water, and sanitary conditions.

Who cut off the water supply to the compound? Who cut it

off from sewers? Who controlled the access of the compound to food? The answer to all three questions is the same: the Federal Bureau of Investigation. To the extent that the children were so abused, the abuser was the FBI itself.

Curiously, a week before the assault, the FBI said that it would not use tear gas on the compound, because it feared for the safety of the children. It had evidence that the adults had gas masks, but the children did not. Yet their operational plan was to pump in gas until the masks failed — which would require *eight hours of continuous gassing*. What did they think would be happening to the people *without* masks — i.e., the children?

Meanwhile, lost in all the commotion was the fact that the cause of the standoff, ATF's February 28 invasion of the Davidian compound, was unjustified. There were three problems with the original raid:

(1) If there was substantial evidence that Koresh or his followers might react violently to any attempt to serve him with a search warrant, why did ATF inform local television stations of the attack two days in advance and invite the stations to send reporters and photographers to accompany the assault? Surely, ATF had to know that seeking publicity in advance of the raid would give notice to those inside the compound, enabling them to prepare for a confrontation.

(2) In the past, Koresh had peacefully submitted to warrants when approached in a normal fashion, without an attack force of a hundred heavily armed men breaking into his home while attack helicopters hovered overhead. Koresh also frequently left the compound. According to the affidavit filed supporting the search warrant, ATF knew that nearly all the guns in the compound were locked up and only Koresh had a key. Why wasn't Koresh served in the conventional fashion? Or, if ATF feared a violent confrontation (as it surely must have — why else would it put together a virtual army to serve the warrant?), why didn't ATF wait to serve the warrant when Koresh was off in Waco

and the Davidians' guns were locked away?

(3) The original ATF attack occurred because the agency suspected Koresh of violating a federal licensing law. Does violation of a licensing law justify an assault of this magnitude?

I have read the search warrant and the affidavit on which it was based. Here is what it contains:

- A report from a sheriff's deputy that one afternoon he heard a "loud explosion in the area" and "as he drove toward the area where he thought the explosion had occurred he observed a large cloud of grey smoke dissipating from the ground";

- An anonymous statement that "Marshal Keith Butler . . . a machinist by trade . . . is associated with Vernon Howell [Koresh's original name] . . . Butler has been arrested on seven (7) occasions since 1984 for unlawful possession of drugs . . . Two of the arrests resulted in convictions . . .";

- Statements that Koresh had reportedly engaged in sex with a variety of young women and had engaged in "child abuse";

- The statements of dissident Davidians and the families of Davidians that the Davidians possessed fully automatic weapons, whose possession requires a federal license;

- The statement by a United Parcel Service driver that Koresh or his representative had paid for C.O.D. items with cash;

- A search of Treasury records, which failed to reveal that the Davidians had acquired a license for the possession of automatic weapons;

- A huge amount of evidence that the Davidians had acquired items that could be used to manufacture weapons requiring licenses (e.g., 30 cardboard tubes). None of the items purchased were illegal and none required licenses;

- The statement of an ATF agent, who testified that on December 4, 1992, he had interviewed Joyce Sparks, a social worker. Sparks told him she had visited the "compound" on April 6, 1992, at which time she spoke to a seven-year-old boy who wanted to grow up so he could get a "long gun" like the older members of the group. "She said that during her conversation with Koresh, he told her that he was the 'Messenger' from God, that the world was coming to an end, and that when he 'reveals' himself the riots in Los Angeles would pale in comparison to what was going to happen in Waco, Texas";

- The statement of Robert Carvenka, a neighbor, that he had heard the sound of automatic weapons fire coming from the Davidian property. Carvenka had served in the military and could identify the sound of automatic weapons fire.

Does this evidence constitute "probable cause" that evidence of a federal crime was concealed on the Davidian property? I have my doubts.

Unless it is now illegal to "associate" with a machinist who has used drugs or to have noise that sounds like "an explosion" and have "smoke" coming from your house, these two bits of evidence seem pretty irrelevant.

The statements about "child abuse" and Koresh's having sex with young women are plainly red herrings, since neither offense violates any federal law. The affidavit does not mention, by the way, that these charges had previously been investigated and dropped by state authorities. It is apparent that the whole "child abuse" issue was brought up only to persuade the judge who issued the warrant and to gain the sympathy and complicity of the American people.

The UPS driver's statement that Koresh had paid cash for C.O.D. items is simply irrelevant: use of cash is not illegal in the United States. Further, C.O.D. deliveries by UPS *must* be paid in cash unless the shipper specifically releases UPS from liability in the event that a check tendered for payment is returned for insufficient funds.

The statements by dissident Davidians are dubious. For one thing, the agent who took the evidence did not cite any reason to believe that any of the witnesses had even passing familiarity with automatic weapons or could distinguish between an AR-15 (a perfectly legal semi-automatic rifle) and an M-16 (an automatic rifle that requires a license). As I understand the law, this renders their testimony virtually worthless. Besides, the testimony of the dissidents ought to be discounted out of simple prudence. They had very strong motivations to cause trouble for Koresh. Consider the following case:

Let us suppose that you and your spouse had a horrible fight, characterized by fervent anger, ugly words, and nasty accusations, resulting in your spouse moving out of the home. Let us suppose your spouse goes to the Bureau of Alcohol, Tobacco, and Firearms and tells them that you are distilling alcohol without a proper license. The ATF checks with your supermarket and learns that you have over the past few years on numerous occasions purchased sugar and on a few occasions purchased yeast, and verifies with your local utility that you have purchased water. You have acquired all the ingredients needed to manufacture alcohol. The ATF also checks the Treasury's records and verifies that you have never acquired a license to make alcohol.

In every detail, this situation is identical to the Davidians': there is testimony from an angry former close associate anxious to cause you trouble, there is evidence that you acquired the means to make a product whose manufacture requires a license, and there is evidence that you had not obtained the license. Is this evidence — "probable cause" — sufficient for you to lose your right to privacy in your home as guaranteed by the fourth amendment?

The statement by Joyce Sparks, the social worker, is both

irrelevant and contains an obvious fabrication. She spoke to Koresh on April 6, yet the Los Angeles riots, which she claims he warned her would be repeated in Waco, did not begin until the end of April.

This leaves the testimony of the neighbor. Here we at last have reasonable testimony that an unlicensed automatic weapon was on the Davidian property. However, the affidavit does not mention the fact that the neighbor had reported the incident to the sheriff, who had investigated the matter and learned that Koresh had a "hell-fire device," which simulated the sound of automatic weapons fire.

Does any of this, or all of it taken together, justify an armed attack?

Why would anyone even consider serving such a faulty warrant? Was ATF motivated by a simple, if wrongheaded, desire to enforce the law? Quite possibly not. In the past few years, critics have targeted the agency for abolition, and in 1993, with Congress searching for ways to cut spending, ATF was especially vulnerable. It is certainly possible that ATF staged the raid to generate good publicity, to prevent its coming under the budgetary knife. CBS's *60 Minutes* reported that a huge sexual harassment scandal at ATF was about to surface when the raid occurred. Perhaps ATF wanted to deflect public attention from this problem.

ATF probably expected its huge show of force to result in a quick surrender by the Davidians. It is not difficult to imagine how the story would play out on television — first on the local news, then on a network "reality program." Stern-faced ATF agents get into their bullet-proof gear, load their weapons, and are transported to the remote location; they surround the fortress and attack; they fire off a few shots, perhaps killing a few evil cultists; they display the guns found at the compound, while an agent explains that there was sufficient firepower for a war (not mentioning that the guns were perfectly legal). A statement would follow from a high-level ATF bureaucrat explaining how the bureau had again protected Americans from civil destruction. And then the payoff: the congresspeople who had been considering abolishing ATF would decide to cut elsewhere in the federal budget.

The ATF did not intend to lose the pitched battle they started, or to kill some of its own agents in the crossfire. They can console themselves by reflecting that they did provide the "deterrence" against joining the Davidians or similar groups that President Clinton had hoped for. ("I hope very much that others who will be tempted to join cults and to become involved with people like David Koresh will be deterred by the horrible scenes they have seen.")

Carnage by Fire

I remain unconvinced that the FBI did not desire a denouement of carnage by fire, if only because past federal attempts to arrest (or serve warrants to) individuals or groups who hold unpopular views and exercise their constitutional right to own firearms have ended with fiery death and the destruction of all evidence that might exonerate the accused. The siege of the Symbionese Liberation Army ended with their incineration. Gordon Kahl, who had survived an ambush of his North Dakota home by U.S. Marshals in February of 1983, fled to Arkansas, where he also was consumed by fire in a confrontation with the FBI in June of that same year.

What would have happened if the FBI hadn't killed Koresh and destroyed all the evidence? We can only surmise. But we can see why the FBI might be concerned. According to Koresh's attorney, David DeGuerin, Koresh was confident that he would be exonerated after the standoff had ended, and was looking forward to defending himself in court.

Consider the case of Randy Weaver, the eccentric right-winger who was involved in a similar standoff in Idaho. Weaver was accused of selling a sawed-off shotgun to a federal under-cover agent but did not show up for his trial in February 1991. Explaining that he believed he could not get a fair trial, he removed himself to an isolated cabin, which he and his family had built from scrap lumber. There was an uneasy standoff, with Weaver and his family living peaceably in their isolated cabin while U.S. Marshals "investigated."

A year and a half later, on August 21, 1992, "The group [of U.S. Marshals] came under fire from the fortresslike Weaver home, apparently without warning, and [U.S. Marshal William] Degan sustained a fatal gunshot wound," according to Henry E. Hudson, director of the U.S. Marshals Service. A siege began. It ended only after Col. Bo Gritz, a war hero who had known Weaver in Vietnam, got the FBI to allow Weaver to surrender peaceably.

Unlike Koresh, Weaver has now had his day in court, and a lot has been learned about the confrontation. Weaver and another survivor of the siege were charged with the murder of Marshal Degan. At the trial, federal authorities were chastised by U.S. District Judge Edward Lodge for fabricating evidence (even faking photographs of the scene of the siege), hiding evidence that the assault on the Weaver family began with the U.S. Marshals firing the first shots, and withholding a wide variety of other evidence from the defense.

The case against Weaver was ridiculous, according to the Associated Press report of May 27, 1993: "Prosecutors have spent several days outlining for jurors their elaborate conspiracy theory, in which Mr. Weaver and his family plotted for a decade to provoke a bloody confrontation with agents of a government they loathed." Apparently, their theory was that in order to provoke a bloody confrontation with federal police, he isolated himself in the wilderness, hoping that the feds would send a bunch of machine-gun-toting agents onto his property to attack him and kill his wife and son.

As the case developed, it emerged that practically every statement coming from federal authorities during the siege of the Weaver cabin was contradicted by subsequent statements from federal authorities and that many "facts" released by those authorities during the siege and dutifully reported in the press were simply false. The statement quoted three paragraphs earlier, for example, contains two falsehoods. The agents did not come under fire "without warning"; in fact, they fired the first shots. The Weaver cabin was not in any way "fortresslike." It was constructed from scrap plywood, 2x4s, and mill ends. As the siege progressed, the lies and contradictions continued: FBI and Marshal spokesmen variously reported that Degan had been killed by a single .223 caliber bullet from an AR-15 and by a .30–06 bullet from an old hunting rifle; the bullet was reported variously to have hit him in the sternum, the neck, and the heart, while he was and was not wearing a bulletproof vest. During the week of August 24–30, federal spokesmen repeatedly told reporters that they were holding back because they feared Weaver's wife might get hurt; it turned out that a federal sniper had shot her dead while she held their infant daughter in her arms. Federal officials repeatedly reported that they were under fire from automatic weapons during the siege, just as they did during the Davidian siege. Yet when they searched the cabin and surrounding area after Weaver's surrender, they found not a single automatic weapon.

If federal agents had managed to kill Weaver and burn over the site, as they did in the cases of Gordon Kahl and David Koresh, they would have saved themselves a lot of embarrassment. Instead, in July of 1993, Weaver was exonerated of all charges relating to the attack on his home.

Waco: Some Truth Comes Out

Reproduced on the opposing page is a letter from President Clinton written to Stephen Cox, who wrote a critical analysis of

THE WHITE HOUSE
WASHINGTON

June 11, 1993

Mr. Stephen Cox
University of California
San Diego, California

Dear Stephen:

Thank you for your letter. I share your concern about the recent situation near Waco, Texas. I was deeply disturbed by the tragic loss of life there. It is especially appalling that innocent children may have suffered at the hands of David Koresh and other members of the Branch Davidian cult.

The compound had been under surveillance for some time, and federal agents determined that cult members were illegally stockpiling weapons. The large number of guns and ammunition and the presence of children near such weapons led agents to begin seizure of the compound. That action provoked the first confrontation, which left four federal agents dead and many other people injured.

After peaceful negotiations had stalled, the appropriate law enforcement agencies, in consultation with Attorney General Janet Reno, formulated a plan that was intended to cause the least harm to cult members while forcing them out of the compound. Tear gas was used because it causes no permanent damage, and it is effective in evacuating the people from a targeted area.

As President, I take full responsibility for the actions of federal agents in Waco. I have ordered a full review of the case to be conducted by both the Justice Department and the Treasury Department to determine what happened and what can be done in the future to handle similar situations better.

Sincerely,

Bill Clinton

the killing of 86 men, women and children near Waco, Texas on April 19 ("Darkness at Noon," *Liberty*, June 1993).

It is an interesting document. Clinton's statement that the children "may have suffered at the hands of David Koresh and other members of the Branch Davidian cult," continues his administration's absurd claim that the "ultimate rationale" (George Stephanopoulos' words) for the attack on the Davidians was that Koresh engaged in child abuse. We've already seen how ridiculous, how far from the truth, this excuse is.

In the second paragraph, Clinton lies again: "The large number of guns and ammunition and the presence of children near such weapons led agents to begin seizure of the compound." According to virtually all claims by ATF about its original attack on the Davidian property, its purpose was to serve a search warrant, not to seize the property. Further, the affidavit supporting the search warrant includes an agent's statement that the guns were kept in a locked location that was kept secret from the children.

In the next paragraph, Clinton makes another curious claim: "Tear gas was used because it causes no permanent damage, and it is effective in evacuating the people from a targeted area." The FBI did not use what is commonly referred to as tear gas, technically known as chloroacetophenone, abbreviated CN. It used something much more powerful: a white powder, technically known as o-chlorobenzalmalononitrile, more commonly called CS.

CS is described by *The Hazardous Chemicals Desk Reference* as "moderately toxic by inhalation" when dispersed into the air. Within seconds, it incapacitates its victims, causing extreme burning, tearing, coughing, difficulty in breathing and chest tightness, blindness, dizziness, vomiting, and nausea. According to Amnesty International, CS has resulted in as many as 80 deaths worldwide, and is "particularly dangerous when used in massive quantities in heavily built-up or populated areas

. . . or when launched directly into homes or other buildings." In 1985, the *Washington Post* reported that Israeli soldiers and police in Gaza had "violated the manufacturer's printed warnings by firing the gas into enclosed areas such as rooms or small courtyards. Most experts agree that such misuses of the gas can be harmful, especially to small children." It is so dangerous that an international treaty prohibits its use in warfare.

The manual used by the U.S. Army for training military police sternly warns: "[CS gas projectiles] are not designed for the direct introduction of a crowd control agent into barricaded buildings. . . . Do not use around . . . places where innocent person may be affected. . . . Do not use where fires may start or asphyxiation may occur. . . . Do not use where a change in wind would cause harm or hamper control operations." The Army's "Civil Disturbances" manual warns: "Generally, persons reacting to CS are incapable of executing organized and concerted actions and excessive exposure to CS may make them incapable of vacating the area."

According to its "Material Data Safety Sheet," published by the Chemical and Biological Defence Agency, CS's flash point is 386° F and its explosive concentration is 0.025 grams/liter (or about 1/1200 of an ounce per quart of air). Pouring CS into enclosed buildings for six hours might very well result in reaching the "explosive concentration" of 0.025 grams/liter, or about 1/1200 of an ounce per quart of air. *The S.W.A.T. Team Manual*, by Robert P. Cappel, is even more explicit: "Be aware of the fact that some gas projectiles will burn while others will explode. Be prepared for the eventuality of a fire."

In sum, employing CS gas against the Davidians could be expected, according to official law enforcement documents and manuals, to prevent the Davidians from vacating the building, to do serious harm to the innocent children, and quite possibly to cause a fire.

This is the chemical the FBI poured into the Davidian buildings for six hours during the assault on April 19, the chemical Clinton claims "was intended to cause the least harm to cult members." As if deliberately trying to contradict the Clinton administration's claim that its "ultimate rationale" for the gas attack was concern for the welfare of the children, the FBI publicly stated that they believed the children inside the buildings had no protection against CS gas.

In his final paragraph, Clinton attempts again to "take full responsibility" for the affair, apparently to try to mitigate his attempts to dodge responsibility during the first hours after the holocaust.

The Cold Monster

Given the extent of the conflagration, and the fact that press sources were kept away from the scene before, during, and after the assault, we may never know how the fire was set. But even if Koresh or a disciple lit the fire, the FBI and the attorney general cannot escape blame for the deaths, any more than the Nazis could escape blame for the deaths of the poor souls they brutalized and tortured in concentration camps until they took their own lives, or the Communists could escape culpability for the brutalized prisoners in their POW camps who died by their own hand.

"The State is the coldest of all cold monsters," Nietzsche told us. Whether Bill Clinton, Janet Reno, the FBI, and the BATF killed the Branch Davidians directly or by driving them to suicide, the case illustrates just how right Nietzsche was.

In Dubious Battle
by R. W. Bradford

The federal government had a $24.8 billion interest payment due on Wednesday, November 15, 1995. This was different from a house payment that a typical family might owe, and not just because it was such a gigantic amount of money. When you or I owe money, we almost always pay it out of current income or savings. But the government has a different way of doing things: It just borrows more. Every time this happens — and it happens every week — the national debt gets a little higher.

But the $24.8 billion due November 15 was different. You see, the U.S. Treasury can borrow money only if it's authorized by Congress. And stingy old Congress had limited Treasury to a measly $4.9 trillion. And Treasury had already borrowed all that.

This happens all the time. The national debt has grown every year for a quarter of a century, and has been growing lately at the rate of about $4 billion a week. So every so often, the administration reluctantly asks Congress to raise the debt authorization "one more time," and Congress does so, on a "temporary" basis.

But things were different this time. The Democratic president and the Republican Congress were locked in a dispute, ostensibly about the whole problem of the budget deficit and the national debt. The president was threatening to veto the new budget (which didn't increase Social Security as much as he wanted it to). No, the budget Congress was enacting did not balance the budget. But it did keep spending increases down to a point where, by Congress' calculation, the budget could be balanced by the second year of the next millennium.

Furthermore, Congress had long ago enacted measures that, in the unlikely event that some future Congress might fail to approve an increase in the debt limit, legally authorized the secretary of the Treasury to take the sort of action to avoid default that a private person facing bankruptcy might take, and might be

139

put in jail for taking. This Congress didn't much care for this sort of legal fraud. So when it authorized another increase in the debt limit, part of the measure removed this wiggle room.

As November 15 approached, Secretary Robert Rubin issued dire warnings about the impending default, not mentioning the anti-default measures at his disposal. Inevitably, these warnings touched off a worry in the currency markets, and the value of the dollar dropped. Why Rubin did this seemed difficult to fathom: Certainly it didn't benefit the United States to have its currency fall into disrepute and its credit rating sink.

If Rubin were to default, the United States would be technically bankrupt and subject to the usual indignities of bankruptcy. This sort of thing occasionally happens to governments, but usually in places like Mexico or Italy. When it happens, the currency of the country goes down the toilet, as investors don't have much interest in lending money to a government that does not repay its debts.

On the morning of Monday, November 13, it was plain that this deadlock would have one of three resolutions:

(1) Congress would cave in and increase the debt limit without taking away Treasury's ability to fudge the books, and the government would go on borrowing an additional $4 billion each week with Congress unable to stop it.

(2) The president would give in and sign the debt limit increase as passed by Congress, which would become a *real* limit.

(3) Neither side would give in, and the U.S. would either default (as Rubin had indicated, causing chaos in financial markets) or Rubin would use the power an earlier Congress had given him to paper over the problem.

At 8:30 a.m., the president ended the suspense. He vetoed the debt authorization and the secretary of the Treasury announced that he would use his legal authority to evade the law. The Treasury manages the retirement funds of federal employees, which are held in the form of government bonds. Naturally, these bonds are an obligation of the United States, and part of the national debt. Rubin tendered the bonds to the Treasury for redemption, thereby lowering the national debt and allowing Treasury to issue more bonds to investors without exceeding the debt limit. The pension funds lent their cash to the Treasury without interest, but this loan is not counted as debt, so it doesn't count as part of the national debt. However, an earlier Congress' legislation promised that the cash will be repaid with interest eventually, so the pension funds will not lose anything. In other words, these actions enable the secretary of the Treasury to borrow money from the government workers' pensions and not include that loan as part of the overall debt.

If a private business were to raid its employees' pension funds to pay its obligations, giving the employees a promise to repay at some vague time in the future, its officers would go to jail. But this, remember, is the U.S. government, a unique institution that is not to be judged by normal standards of decency or honesty.

Upon Rubin's announcement, the dollar rallied, the price of gold dropped $4.00 and peace returned to financial markets. But it's a funny kind of peace. Speculators are a little upset, a little worried. The market isn't racked with the pain of an ulcer, but it is a bit queasy.

No one really seemed to know just how much wiggle room Treasury had. How many billions of dollars could be shifted about to paper over the problem of the relentless need for $4 billion or so per week to cover the deficit?

It turns out Treasury's wiggle room is more like a wiggle stadium. On Wednesday, less than three days after Secretary Rubin had been speaking gravely about default, he announced that the Treasury's crack team of attorneys, working around the clock while Rubin was publicly worrying, had discovered sufficient legal authorization for another year's borrowing that wouldn't count as real debt. So no matter how much Congress wants to stop the dollar hemorrhage, it can't do so for at least until the 1996 elections are over. Which, it turns out, is a critical point.

The Role of Politics

During the congressional battle over the the creation of Medicare in 1964, the Democrats bought television ads showing a man putting three quarters into a pay phone while the announcer intoned that the cost of Medicare would be only 75¢ per week. The implication was that it would be downright immoral to oppose a measure that would solve the health problems of the elderly at such a low cost. And so Medicare was enacted, at a cost of $6.00 per recipient per month, half paid by the recipient, half paid by the taxpayer.

By 1995, the effects of inflation and subsidy had driven up the monthly cost from $6.00 to $146.35. Congress had responded to the rising cost by decreasing the portion paid by the recipient from 50% to 31.5%, so now the elderly pay premiums of $46.10 per month (deducted from their Social Security check), while the taxpayer chips in $100.25.

Even this seemed too high to the elderly, who successfully lobbied an earlier Congress to give them an even larger subsidy. And so, as the law now stands, as of 1996 the elderly will pay only 25% of the cost of their visits to doctors' offices, with taxpayers picking up 75%. With another year of price inflation fueled by subsidy, the total cost of the coverage increased by 16.1%, but the cost to the recipient would decrease to $42.50, with the taxpayer now picking up $127.41.

This increased subsidy seemed like a poor idea even to Bill Clinton, who proposed in 1993 that it be repealed to help bring spending under control. So when the Republicans tried their hand at cutting government spending this year, they naturally included this measure. Under the budget passed by Congress, the premium deducted from the elderly's Social Security check in

1996 would have risen to $53.50, an increase of $7.40. Happily, the average Social Security payment will rise by $18.00 per month, so the net amount received would still increase. Since the president had supported this measure in the past, it seemed non-controversial.

But the Republicans had underestimated Bill Clinton's lust for power and his willingness to adjust his beliefs to gain voter support.

The president wants to score some points with old people and increase his chances of re-election. On the theory that old people vote their pocketbooks, Clinton figures that if he can convince them the Republicans will mean less loot, they'll quickly become Democrats. And Bill Clinton can no more pass up an opportunity to win votes than he could pass up an opportunity to "get to know" Gennifer Flowers.

So the president took to the airwaves, denouncing the very proposal he had made in 1993. He vetoed the budget. "I *want* to balance the budget," he said. "But I don't want to destroy Medicare." The Republican plan to do away with the increased Medicare subsidy is an attempt "to impose huge hikes in Medicare premiums. . . . I am fighting it today. I will fight it tomorrow. I will fight it next week and next month," he roared to the television cameras. "I will fight until we get a budget that is fair to all Americans."

On his television show, Rush Limbaugh aired a videotape of the 1993 version of Bill Clinton proposing the measure he now indignantly denounced. *The Wall Street Journal* ran a news article, pointing out that the difference between the Republican proposal and the president's was only $11.00 per month for Social Security recipients, not the draconian difference suggested by the president's claims. But Limbaugh is widely perceived as a GOP apologist, and both he and the *WSJ* were preaching to the choir.

And the president bought television spots, showing a middle-aged couple at their kitchen table. What can we do about Grandma, now that Medicare is slashed? "She's . . . she's my mother," says the woman. Tears well up in the eyes of the actors, and in living rooms across the nation. Needless to say, the ad didn't mention the cost of Grandma's Medicare coverage would rise only $7.40 per month under the GOP proposal, or that the couple already pays, via payroll deduction, about $180 per month to support Medicare, and that this figure will inevitably rise if the president prevails.

Suddenly, Bill Clinton was rising in the polls, which also showed that most voters blamed the budget crisis on the Republicans. Clinton had at last found an issue that was working for him.

The Republicans read the same polls, and caved in to the president on Medicare on Wednesday, only one day after the crisis had come to a head. Now, they figured, the president would agree to balance the budget in seven years, a plan using the nonpartisan Congressional Budget Office's economic projections, and sign their budget, which would allow "non-essential" government offices to reopen.

But Clinton was not about to accept their surrender, not while his popularity was rising. "You are in a situation where the White House is clearly emboldened," said former Democratic senator Paul Tsongas. "They [sic] see this as their ticket to 1996."

"The longer this goes on," Democratic pollster Geoff Garin said, "the more it gives advantage" to Clinton. "The public gets to understand that what this [crisis] means in reality is higher Medicare premiums and less Medicaid, less funding for nursing homes, less funding for student aid."

So Clinton said the Republicans would have to give up more. Any plan to balance the budget must be based on the perpetually rosy (and uniformly inaccurate) projections of his Office of Management and Budget. And it would have to ensure no cuts in entitlement programs.

By this time, you will recall, Secretary of the Treasury Rubin had found a way to keep the government running, more or less, for another year without the permission of Congress. Clinton figured he could ignore Congress until the election, gaining in popularity all the time. He just might be a two-term president.

Delightfully unencumbered by any beliefs or principles, Clinton held the upper hand. On Sunday, November 19, the Republicans caved in. In exchange for Clinton's "commitment" to balance the budget within seven years, using a plan that "basically" follows CBO projections, they agreed to keep entitlement funding at "adequate" levels and to authorize an increase in the debt ceiling that will suffice until December 13. And federal workers, unlike workers laid off in private industry, would be paid at their regular wages for the six days they were furloughed. The agreement, CNN reported, gave the president "room to maneuver."

And so this battle in the Budget War went to the Democrats, though Gingrich and Dole tried to portray it as a Republican victory. Clinton had turned the Republican attack back on them, forcing a retreat. He had committed to nothing, while getting the Republicans to back down on key issues and gaining in the polls.

But there will be more battles, perhaps as soon as December 13. The Budget War is not over yet.

The Prospects for a Balanced Budget

For the first time in the memory of any person born since World War II, Congress seems to be trying to get government spending under control. This goes contrary to the whole conventional political process, which elevates every problem to the status of an emergency to be used to justify more spending, while at the same time calling for a balanced budget. The old system sat very well with voters, who like spending and like balanced budgets but aren't very crazy about tax increases.

Of course, it is impossible to raise spending, cut taxes, and erase a budget deficit all at the same time. The way around this thorny problem is to solve the last problem in the future, by making economic projections that show things getting better (so tax revenue will rise sharply) and problems going away (so spending can shrink, or at least not grow very much). Lo and behold, when the future comes, the deficit is even larger.

Of course, even those with the most negligible understanding of economics can see the silliness of this. When the government subsidizes an activity (say, provision of medical care to the indigent or elderly), demand for the activity is increased and the cost rises rather than declines. And, of course, government officials never cease to discover new crises that require additional spending and bigger staffs and more power. This presents no real problem: The politicians simply increase the deficit, and enact a plan to reduce and eliminate it during the next five years. The White House has a special bureau, its Office of Management and Budget, whose sole function is to cook up projections that justify the new plans to balance the budget during the period three to seven years later.

So the deficit has continued to grow and the national debt has exploded in the past 40 years, while every president and every Congress has promised to reduce or eliminate the deficits. Every year for the past quarter-century, the government has spent more money than it has taken in. The federal debt has tripled in the past ten years. And it tripled in the ten years before that. Today, the federal government is about $4.9 trillion in debt.

The budget process has become a ritual. Congress enacts and the president signs a budget with a huge deficit, at the same time revealing a multi-year plan to balance the budget. Within a few years, the plan is obsolete, as revenues have proved lower than expected and expenses higher. The need for a balanced budget is agreed upon, and a new budget is drawn up. Once again, the current year has a huge deficit. But once again, spending and revenue for future years are projected to converge into equality.

Ostensibly to break this cycle of ever-increasing deficits, the Gramm-Rudman Act was signed into law in 1985. It outlawed the deficit. But Congress found ways around the law, and the deficits continued to grow.

Things looked different after 1994. Virtually every Republican candidate for Congress signed a "Contract with America," making an explicit promise to balance the budget. Swept into control after being out of power in the House for 40 years, the new Republicans quickly proposed and passed a balanced budget amendment.

This was the first battle of the Budget War, and the Republicans almost won it. But they failed to get enough Democratic votes for the necessary two-thirds majority in the Senate. This was not necessarily a bad thing: There were problems with the amendment's wording that could have made it just another toothless weapon. At any rate, the battle was a draw: The Democrats had fended off the Republican knockout punch, but the Republicans had mustered large majorities in both houses and scored a clear victory with the voters.

Now the Democrats have won a clear victory in the second battle of the Budget War. The Republicans claim to have learned from this defeat, and remain determined, they say, to continue the fight.

Before you conclude that the Republicans will stand up to the president and win the war, take a look at the graph on this page. It shows the budget deficit for every year between 1936 and 1992.

Most people think the Democrats are the party of deficit spending, while the Republicans are the party of balanced budgets. But that is not the case. Indeed, to judge from this graph, the major cause of deficits is Republican presidents (who are marked with shaded areas). Eisenhower was pretty good, but Nixon, Reagan, and Bush were terrible.

But it is not fair to blame this entirely on them. These Republican presidents had Democratic Congresses, after all. And it is Congress that enacts the budget, not the president.

Nor are wars the major cause of the huge debt. There were big deficits during World War II. But the Korean War resulted in no deficits at all, and the Vietnam War deficits were pretty small.

The real cause of the huge deficit is the enormous increase in entitlement spending that began under Johnson, was expanded by subsequent presidents, and has now become a part of American life. Of the $885 billion in entitlement spending in 1995, only $140 billion went to the poor. The rest went to programs for the middle class, in the form of Medicare, student loans, farm subsidies, Social Security, veterans' benefits, and a hundred other programs.

The middle-class voter is happy to cut programs that benefit the poor or the rich. But I doubt very many middle-class voters want to cut programs that benefit themselves. They don't mind balancing the budget on someone else's back. But when push comes to shove, they'd rather live with perpetual deficits than give up their government subsidies.

It's going to take more than rollbacks of increased Medicare subsidies to balance the budget. If you think voters are upset now, wait until someone proposes substantial *cuts* in their handouts. If the Republican resolution to roll back a minor Medicare premium cut evaporates after a week's worth of television spots and a few phony righteous harrumphs from the president, what are the chances they will find the resolve to enact actual cuts in middle-class entitlements?

Very slim, I am afraid. Maybe I'm wrong about this. I *hope* that I am. But I suspect middle-class voters will react as they have in the past, and Republican congresspeople will react as Republican presidents have reacted in the past. I wouldn't make any bets that the budget will be balanced in the foreseeable future.

Meanwhile, I shall celebrate the recent government "shutdown." My local congressman went on television to enumerate the hardships it was causing — the Smithsonian was closed, the Washington Monument was shut down, the IRS wasn't answering its help lines — and concluded absurdly, "Now we can see just how much we need government."

Yeah, right. A couple tourist attractions closed, no "help" from the IRS . . . how can we go on? If nothing else, the budget crisis should help Americans understand just how unimportant the federal government is to their real lives. Now there's an accomplishment!

All in the Tribe
by Stephen Cox

In mid-November of 1995, when the balanced-budget war between the president and Congress was getting hot, Rush Limbaugh revealed to his audience one of those strange and annoying "contradictions" that opinion polls are always turning up. A majority of Americans, or so it appeared, supported a balanced budget; but a majority of Americans also resented any specific proposals to balance it. They wanted no cuts in "Social Security," no cuts in "Medicare," no cuts in "defense," no cuts in — whatever.

At this news, Rush's audience turned ugly. Caller after caller denounced, not just President Clinton, but the American people, who were immoral, irresponsible, hypocritical, and every other bad thing you could think of. Rush tried to quell the antipopulist frenzy, but at last even he got worn down, ending the afternoon with fainter and fainter references to the people's temporary confusion, the possibility that they would gradually come to their senses, the continued need to fight the good fight, and so forth.

None of his callers seemed convinced. It just didn't make sense to them. How can the American people want something and not want it at the same time, without being, well, nothing but a bunch of hypocrites? And the callers clearly had reason on their side — at least in their analysis of other people's political and moral behavior. The polls did imply that people wanted to get certain political goods without paying for them or taking the responsibility of thinking about what that might mean.

But Rush's callers were not so good at analyzing a field of behavior that is related to, but not the same as, politics, a field that is more appropriately studied by the amateur anthropologist than by the amateur moralist or policy wonk.

I refer to the behavior of the tribe.

A tribe is a group of people held together not just by common descent or location but by shared conceptions of a common identity, conceptions represented in symbols and realized in symbolic action.

Notice that these are immaterial and often wholly impractical considerations. Think of the difference between watching football and being a fan of some particular football team. One might understand the game perfectly, one might enjoy it keenly, one might even make profitable bets on it, but one might still stop short of being a fan. Being a fan of the Buffalo Bills does not imply that one has any practical interest in the fate of Buffalo, N.Y., or any clear idea of where Buffalo, N.Y., happens to be — much less any clear idea of who Buffalo Bill was or what buffaloes have to do with any of the above. A fan is someone who wears a buffalo on his cap. Wearing it is his form of symbolic identification with other fans.

To be a fan, one does not have to believe or think about much of anything. One does not have to weigh the evidence and decide that Buffalo has an excellent team and should therefore be especially interesting to watch this Sunday. A fan *hopes* that his team will be good this year, but he will watch it play, no matter what, and he will yell at the television set, as if it could answer him. He knows, by the way, that it will not answer. He is not crazy; he is simply expressing his tribal identity in symbolic action.

Now, let us apply this little anthropological analogy to the problem of America's allegedly hypocritical populace. What are the political insignia of the American tribe? For the past two generations or so the insignia have included Social Security (an established government program), Medicare (an established government program), a strong military (an established government program), and a balanced budget (a pious wish). These are all artifacts of America, symbols of American power and good will. Anyone who favors these things is a fan of America. We are *for* these things, because we are *for* our team; and who knows, perhaps it will win. In any event, we are *for* it. We are for it *all*.

Tribal identity is not an especially rational and not an entirely static thing. There are tribes that began as hunters and gatherers and had unto themselves the gods of hunters and gatherers. When they became agricultural, they made for themselves other gods, without entirely discarding the old ones. To determine which gods are worshiped at the moment, and how they are worshiped, an anthropologist needs to rely on something more than abstract reasoning about what arguments should impel the tribe to maximize its religious utilities. Instead, the anthropologist will consult the experts who are in charge of manipulating the symbols of the tribe. He will consult the witch doctors. These are the people who select the symbols that hold the tribe to its identity. Their interest in the matter is very strong. If they exalt the right symbols, they will be able to maintain their own exalted social role.

On January 3, I consulted some of the most experienced witch doctors in America. I observed a ritual press conference of the Democratic Party leadership.

The topic was the various un-American things that Republican congressmen were doing. The chief complaint was that the Republicans had shut down "the government," pending President Clinton's agreement to a balanced budget plan. Subsidiary complaints involved the delayed paychecks of federal employees and the imminent starvation of "senior citizens who can't get Meals on Wheels."

A political analyst might immediately decide — and would be right in deciding — that all of this consisted of so many promises of material benefits to be given in exchange for votes. People who bank on government were being told to exert their influence in behalf of the Democratic Party. No anthropological insight was necessary to penetrate this political stratagem. But without anthropological insight, the Democratic leadership would be unable to mobilize the majority of Americans who do not get Meals on Wheels or receive a federal paycheck — the majority of Americans who, in fact, would probably be happy to donate a few bucks a year for Meals on Wheels if they had any bucks to spare after the government employees get through with them.

To mobilize this majority, a display of pure symbolism was offered. A symbolic history was created, and along with it symbolic enemies and a symbolic drama of suffering and salvation.

Speaking of the Republican-inspired budget "crisis," Rep. Richard Gephardt (D–Mo.), minority leader of the House, contended that "for the first time in American history" millions of people were "being held hostage by extremists." It is pointless to seek any historical reality that might lie behind this historical myth.

Of course, you could try arguing about it. You could try recalling, to cite one obvious example, the millions of blacks who were once held in slavery by people whose conduct might be considered, by modern standards, somewhat extreme. You could try speculating that American politics was "held hostage" by such "extremists" throughout the first half of the nineteenth century, that the crises of 1850 and 1860–1865 were a good deal more serious than the supposed crisis of 1996, and so forth. But you would be missing Gephardt's point, which was to invite the worship of a tribal god ("American history") and the reviling of a tribal devil ("extremism").

And what, may we ask, is "extremism," in this particular era of the life of our tribe? Extremists, Rep. Gephardt declared, are people who believe that "government is the enemy."

By this he meant the freshman Republicans, who had just rejected Senator Dole's advice that "enough is enough" and it's time to compromise with the Democrats. Gephardt lauded Dole for saying that. A good witch doctor always extends professional courtesy to another, and witch doctors are by no means confined to the Democratic Party. But Gephardt's insight went beyond the divination of good and evil spirits. It involved the power of symbols that are self-reflexive and circular. What the extremists failed to understand, he said, was that in America "the government" is "us"; for *this* reason, he implied, anyone who opposes "the government," even for a week or a month, is not one of "us" and should have nothing to say about anything that *we* do.

We are the Church and the Church is us, and apart from the Church, what would we be? "He that gathereth not with me, scattereth."

The equation of "government" and "us" has no literal meaning; it is entirely symbolic, and it is symbolic not of any political mechanism by which power is wielded but of a saving state of identification between oneself and all the other good adherents of the team. "WE are FAM-I-*LY*!": so goes the old disco song, often sung in athletic stadiums.

It was the deployment of this kind of symbolism that frightened the Republicans into relenting on January 5 and "reopening the government." The voters — who, after all, had little evidence, given the records of both political parties, to believe that politics is anything more than a game — were telling pollsters that they were slightly more impressed by the war cries of the Democrats than by those of the Republicans. The Republicans got scared and left the field, leaving their opponents to crow about their supposed superiority as a governing party.

In fact, the Democrats were simply playing a game of psychic intimidation, relying on the immense pile of statist symbolism that the American tribe has inherited from the past few generations of welfare liberalism. Americans have long been taught to regard the welfare state as Rep. Gephardt evidently wishes to regard it, as a divine entity in which everyone mystically participates. (People like Thoreau may have had trouble believing that the government is "us," but he was sort of an oddball, wasn't he?)

Since this image of the state, moreover, is nothing but symbolism, it is highly susceptible to manipulation. Images can easily be revised to agree with contemporary fashions. Times being what they are, government's symbolic image is no longer that of a benignly distant figure ("General Washington") or even that of a demanding patriarch ("Uncle Sam Wants *You*!"). It has been altered to that of the kindly and succoring aunt ("Meals on Wheels") — a busybody, perhaps, but she means well; and we couldn't really do without her. This is the Age of Caring, and caring is naturally associated with images of domesticity.

Such images were very cleverly manipulated by that old smoothie of the *New York Times*, Russell Baker, in his column of January 6. Baker's ruling metaphor for the budget crisis was that of conflict within a family, the kind of family whose existence is imperilled by the childish or insane behavior of certain members (you know who). Baker was troubled by the lack of kindness that the Republican "radicals" had shown to their sweet old uncle, Senator Dole, whose attempt at compromise with Clinton they had rudely rebuffed.

Dole had, of course, acted in accordance with the mores of the tribe, as currently defined: "He is a government man, trained by years of Washington experience in the art of making government work." His Republican adversaries were distinguished by their gross impiety to the household gods: "The Gingrich people . . . profess to loathe government, and most probably mean it."

You can imagine how trying such a religious conflict can be for a family. Uncle Bob had been "repudiated and embarrassed," "cavalierly abused by his own people." "Play[ing] cut-throat in the budget quarrel," they came "out to get" poor Senator Dole. The whole thing was a blot on the history of the tribe. The Republican radicals, Baker declared with the priestly smugness of the *Times* at its best,

> believe their demand for a balanced budget in seven years makes them champions of a principle too high to allow for compromise. Most things in American life, of course, are the result of compromise — even including the location of Washington, D.C., and the

structure of the Congress itself.

Still, zealous devotion to principle is the American style this year. See the right-to-life and "militia" movements. The rule of governing used to be, "Half a loaf is better than none." No more. Now it is, "I want the whole loaf, and I want it now. . . ."

During the great government "shutdown," the ineffable CNN Headline News broadcast incessant "interviews" with "American citizens" — usually government employees — who explained the event with references to Congress' "childish" refusal to compromise. But it took a genius like Russell Baker to surround this domestic bad conduct with an appropriately mythologized history.

His performance was masterly. Note his juxtaposition of airy generality ("most things in American life") and arcane specificity ("the location of Washington, D.C."), all sanctified by that confident "of course." *Obviously,* everyone who understands American history understands the importance of compromise; if you don't understand it, you're not an authentically concerned American but a mere disrupter of the tribe. Maybe you're a militia member! Maybe you're about to throw a bomb! Maybe you oppose abortion!

If you feel like quibbling about this, Baker just hasn't the time for you. You might be tempted to ask, If compromise is the virtue of our tribe, why did we put Abraham Lincoln, rather than James Buchanan, on the five-dollar bill? But by the time you have the sense to bring this up, Baker has depicted you as a squalling little brat who is trying to snatch that other half-a-loaf from the rest of your presumably hungry family.

Yet for the boldest experiment in the renovation and domestication of tribal symbolism, one must return to January 3 and the remarks of Tom Daschle (D–S.D.), minority leader of the Senate. Like his colleague, Rep. Gephardt, Daschle knows that the most powerful images are often those that unite seeming oppositions. Gephardt declared the mystery of the perfect union of government and people; Daschle decreed that the government is victim as well as savior. He did not just mention the multitudes who look up daily to their government for life and health; he invoked the sufferings of the poor government itself. He invoked the pain of those hundreds of thousands of federal employees "whose lives have been shaken" by the cruelty of Congress.

Again, the factual referent of such symbolism would be far to seek. The paychecks of federal employees had been slightly delayed; many of these employees had also suffered from a free vacation. So what? But the effect of Daschle's poetic remarks was the symbolic identification of government — every atom and speck of government — with the life-tremors of our tribe in the intimacy of its domestic moments. We all know what it means when our lives are *shaken*: we get a divorce, we lose a friend, we lose a job, we try to save ourselves from some horrible addiction, we learn that we have contracted cancer. Just so, according to Senator Daschle's imagery, is it with government. Government is people, people like us, people whose *lives* have been *shaken*. We must save its life, as we would save our own.

At some distance behind such words we can discover the familiar symbols of Christianity: the Good Samaritan, salvation through sacrifice, the sufferings of the wounded healer. One remembers Clinton's decision to call his political program "the New Covenant." The old religion remains — at just the right distance for subliminal exploitation. That distance can be measured by the degree to which Americans have left formal and doctrinal religion and identified themselves with a government that has assumed many quasi-religious functions.

It's well worth noting that wherever formal and doctrinal religion has roused itself, it has struggled to reclaim its old insignia from government, to reclaim the charities, schools, and moral responsibilities that used to be the peculiar possessions of the church. That is why proponents of big government always invoke the spectre of "the religious Right" when they need some symbols of diablerie.

But now we are in the realm of competing treatments of symbolism. The difference between twentieth-century Americans and some primitive tribe is that a complex society has many possible ways of expressing its identity. The welfare liberals' incessant invocation of the American "family" is a directly competitive response to the religious conservatives' invocation of "family values" as the characteristic expression of the tribe.

The welfare liberals' other main competition comes from the rationalists, the people who are unimpressed by any but a practical and literal approach to politics. The rationalists are demystifiers. Their strategy is to reveal the emptiness of all mere symbols of the state. The rationalists have demonstrated, with miles of statistics, with a real knowledge of history, and with perfect truth, that "we" are not the government, that government isn't our kindly relative, that government, in fact, doesn't give a damn about much of anything but its self-perpetuation, and that the welfare of the nation is largely the product of individuals' ability to keep themselves out of the clutches of government.

These tactics have had some effect, at least in increasing the self-confidence of the rationalists themselves. The problem is that the rationalists usually cast themselves as mere watchers of the game, disdainful of the fans and their peculiar folkways. In fact, these rationalists (or I should say *we* rationalists, since virtually all libertarians are like this) would probably be happy enough just to call the game off. Why fuss around with "symbols" and "identities," when you can simply demonstrate that Social Security is a disaster and that if we want to make some progress we should start phasing it out, no matter what most of the old people think?

This approach has gotten us no closer to ending Social Security.

Perhaps it is time for a more anthropologically-friendly

approach. I am not calling for us to become our own witch doctors. We don't have the experience or the cunning to do that; and besides, as Mr. Nixon once remarked, "That would be wrong." What is most necessary is for us to link our own political positions with the hitherto misused symbols of American identity.

Begin with a list of the adjectives that Americans like to apply to themselves as a nation: powerful, efficient, healthy, caring, responsible. Think about the ways in which every political proposal you advance could associate itself with that composite image of the tribe, and give that image the substantial relevance to good politics that the witch doctors would deny it.

If you're talking about Social Security, make sure that people know the facts — how much it costs, how little they are likely to get from it, how much it hurts the economy. But make sure to insist on how much wealthier, how much more independent and secure our parents and grandparents would be if they had the power to invest 15% of their income privately. If you're arguing against the state's continual military interventions in the affairs of other countries, don't just review the statistics about how much these expeditions cost, or scoff at the idea that America constantly needs to demonstrate its "leadership." Dwell on the traditional image of America as a country that exerts moral leadership by exhibiting self-restraint. (You might recall how the founding fathers viewed such matters.) If somebody advocates gun control as a way of preventing the deaths of thousands of innocent people, don't just denounce politicians for using wildly erroneous statistics on this subject to make themselves seem "caring." Show that you care about the poor and elderly people whose guns give them protection that police forces cannot or will not supply.

And for God's sake, when somebody makes an inane remark about democratic rights in the economy, don't immediately quote H.L. Mencken to the effect that democracy is the theory that the people know what they want and deserve to get it good and hard. Nothing against Mencken, but you'll get farther if you talk about how wonderful it would be if we all had the power to make our own economic decisions, without interference from the government.

You see what I mean; you can think of your own examples.

Years ago, I asked my friend Bill Bradford what he thought of the "tribal rock musical" *Hair*, and he said, "I don't know; I guess I'm just not tribal." That's pretty much the way that I feel, too. Libertarians are not a particularly tribal folk. (Come to think of it, though, a lot of us do get an irrational thrill when the local Libertarian candidate for Congress receives 6% of the vote. That may not mean much in strictly political terms, but *it's still our team*.) However that may be, it is not always a concession to collectivism to speak the tribal language. T.S. Eliot writes about the need

> To purify the dialect of the tribe
> And urge the mind to aftersight and foresight.

You can't purify the dialect if you can't see the point in using it.

My Dinner With Slick Willie
by Douglas Casey

A quarter century has passed sinced I graduated from Georgetown University, so, naturally, some of my classmates organized a class reunion. One of my fellow students had risen to a position of prominence, and invited the reunion into his spacious home. That student's name is Bill Clinton. The reunion had the highest percentage turnout in Georgetown's history, and was also the largest sitdown dinner in the history of the White House.

The invitation to the soireé instructed us to R.S.V.P. with our Social Security numbers. It seems the White House didn't want any of Bill's old classmates around unless they had run security checks on them. Oh well, if you want dinner with Bill, you gotta pay the price.

For entertainment, the program had panel discussions on health care, the economy, foreign relations, and social trends. I sat on the social trends panel and was suitably outrageous, much to the apparent delight of the audience.

But the health care panel was more interesting to me. Reading *Doonesbury*, I've come to learn that the White House is populated by a bunch of kids in their 20s and early 30s who all want to control the fate of the nation while they grow up. The Billary person on the health care panel was a prim, athletic-looking, short-haired young lady of 27 years, identified as Hillary's chief assistant in this area. She reminded me of nothing so much as a small velociraptor — alert, eyes darting everywhere.

What she said were forgettable party-line generalities. But it was apparent that, although she made a show of listening, a cold plastic veneer of a smile covering her face, the young velociraptor absolutely knew best and was being polite for the sake of show. Scary.

161

That night, at the White House, I had a photo op with Bill. I offered him a friendly "Hi, Bill, how you doin'?" He responded with a sincere "Hello, Doug, how are you?" I don't recall ever having met him in school, so he must have gotten my name by completely unobtrusively looking at my nametag. I was impressed.

The other entertainment that evening was Chuck Berry. Which meant that another old friend of mine, Bob Baldari, would be at the party. Bob is a civil rights attorney in real life, but he plays keyboards with Chuck whenever he gets the chance. I had learned that Bob was invited a few weeks earlier, when an FBI agent showed up at my house to ask questions about him. The agent was decked out in a bomber jacket and Ray-Bans, just like the G-men in *Midnight Run* — the ones Robert De Niro asks, "Did your mothers dress you all alike? Fashions by Foster Grant?" It seems Bob once had a problem with the law, something about possessing some of the herb that Bill Clinton smoked but didn't inhale. The FBI guy asked me some questions about Bob, but I wasn't much help to him. There was only one G-Man, and I figured I couldn't be in trouble unless there were at least two of them, and as a matter of principle I don't talk to the authorities about my friends.

Well, Bob was allowed to perform, no thanks to me. It turns out that Chuck Berry threatened to skip the party if he couldn't have his keyboard man there. But they weren't taking any chances: Bob was shadowed by a suit that night, at very close range. Like two feet.

Of course, the place was crawling with grim-looking thugs dressed in cheap suits with buldges under the arms and little earphones sticking out of their heads. Only their dark glasses were missing; I suppose they are dispensible indoor at night. I'm sure they did a good job of keeping the president alive, though they didn't stop any of my classmates from pocketing a bunch of presidential silverware as souvenirs.

Bill gave a short speech, with everyone clapping and cheering uproariously at every opportunity — except the two times Bill made policy references. Then, the applause was subdued and polite. Everyone who knew Bill liked him well enough, but few supported his policies; Georgetown was a politically and socially conservative school in the '60s. It's only natural, though, that everyone felt better about him after the party than they did before. Just being there made you feel like a privileged insider, one of his team. And nobody, including myself, likes to speak ill of someone who's hosted you in his house, even if you're the one who bought it for him. A good time was had by all, perhaps even Hillary, who sat near Bill but was surrounded by three or four pert velociraptors at all times.

The next day, I ran into Tim Chorba, another classmate from Georgetown Class of '68. These days he's a partner with powerful Washington lobbyist/law firm Patton, Boggs, & Blow and a real insider in the Clinton administration, so I figured I'd ask him about the cheap-suited guy who stuck to Bob Baldari like glue during the entire evening. He went into his bureaucratic mumbo-jumbo mode, giving me a lengthy explanation of the importance of protecting the president from people who had actually inhaled and are thereby risks to the Free World.

Then he paused a moment, and looked puzzled. "The way I understood it," he finally said, "there was supposed to be a security guy on you, too."

What's Next?
by R.W. Bradford

Contrary to the political consultants, news spinners, and media commentators, the 1994 Republican landslide was neither a "sea change" nor a "revolution." It was a public rejection of the established political religion, a rejection so profound that it shocked the political establishment and the media elite. But the public made no profession of a new faith, nor did it reject political faith altogether.

The Clintons' brand of statism is finished. Statism itself is not.

The old faith actually began to subside long ago. In 1964, the Republican Party briefly stopped saying "me too" to the welfare state (though not, alas, to the warfare state) and chose Barry Goldwater as its presidential candidate. The intellectual establishment recognized Goldwater for the revolutionary he was and vilified him in the rankest terms. After a brutal smear campaign, Lyndon Johnson was elected with 61% of the popular vote, which he and the statolatrous establishment took as a mandate to accelerate government power, in the form of vast increases in domestic spending (the Great Society) and international intervention (the Vietnam War).

The public reacted against the extremism of Johnson's programs. In 1968, Johnson's hand-picked successor got only 43% of the vote, a decline of 30% in just four years. But the winning candidate made no challenge to the ideological status quo, and the size and power of government continued to grow during the administrations of welfare state Republicans Richard Nixon and Gerald Ford and "moderate" Democrat Jimmy Carter.

Still, it was obvious that things were changing during the 1970s. In 1971, the Libertarian Party was founded, and by 1976 it had established itself on the political landscape as a vocal challenger to the political faith. In 1978, California voters passed a

164

radical tax limitation measure, despite the direst of threats from the media, politicians, and intellectuals, groups who benefited from the growth of government and whose piety was undiminished.

In 1980, the Republicans nominated Ronald Reagan for the presidency. Reagan eloquently opposed the growth of government and proposed to reduce its size and power, cut taxes, and increase individual freedom. He was elected in a landslide, and brought in a GOP majority in the Senate — the first time the party had enjoyed a majority in either house of Congress since 1954. Reagan pursued his program, but with only limited success. Everywhere it ran into two problems:

(1) Welfare-state Democrats controlled the House of Representatives, and welfare-state Republicans among the GOP majority in the Senate limited Reagan's ability to enact his program.

(2) The American people were very reluctant to give up the favors that government seemed to have bestowed on them.

Reagan dealt with both of these difficulties by compromising. Because he believed the greatest threat to American liberty was international Communism, he made increasing the military power of the United States his top priority. To get Democrats to agree to increase military spending, he agreed to accept increases in spending for social programs.

Reagan made a similar compromise with the American people. When he broached the idea of cutting middle-class welfare spending — programs such as Social Security and guaranteed student loans — many voters reacted with horror. So Reagan limited his free-market reforms to a few areas: he tried to privatize a few government programs, lifted price controls on oil, opposed increases in the minimum wage, fought gun control, broke the back of the powerful air traffic controllers' union, and made a few other pro-market moves. But he left most institutions of the welfare state alone, allowing them to continue to grow. In some cases, such as the EEOC, he even actively increased their power.

Almost every government program benefits someone, if only the people who are given money by it. Only one form of government activity has no popular support: taxation. So Reagan ended up cutting taxes and increasing spending. And everything seemed nice. Americans got the "benefits" of higher spending without paying the costs of higher taxes. There were student loans, matching funds, grants for public buildings, summer job programs, weapons systems, porkbarrel projects galore. To pay for all this, we borrowed money. Our kids could pay it back. Some day. The program "worked." We were all living beyond our means, thanks to the fact that our government had borrowed over $1,500,000,000,000 and lavished it on us.

Democrats had always had trouble getting away with this sort of thing. Before the Reagan years, whenever Democratic presidents proposed huge budget deficits, Republicans and conservative southern and western Democrats would complain that we were mortgaging our future, that the program was fiscally unsound, that in the end there would be a disaster.

But Reagan's followers were reluctant to criticize their leader. They were tired of losing elections, and Ronald Reagan had shown them that if only they would stop complaining about deficit spending and go along with the program, they could win for a change.

Americans were prosperous and happy, as prosperous and happy as a family that borrows against the value of its home and spends the money on parties. But like that family, we were in danger of losing our way of life, as the national debt ballooned, and the interest payments skyrocketed.

In 1988, the voters elected Reagan's vice president, George Bush, to the presidency, thanks partly to the good will Americans had for Reagan and partly to the Democrats' foolish decision to nominate an unreconstructed big-government, high-tax liberal. In 1990, Bush raised taxes and lost the support of those who had elected him. In 1992, he went down in defeat.

Americans Wake Up

But in 1994, things were different. Republicans had adopted a new theme, and proclaimed it in virtually all their races: the old faith isn't working. The old system of raising taxes, increasing regulation, and solving every problem by throwing money at it has wasted billions of dollars, left our streets unsafe, strangled the American economy, and created a Congress whose members live like oriental potentates while ignoring the people. The Republicans wrote a "Contract With America" that promised to address these problems in the first 100 days of a Republican Congress. And almost everywhere, the Republicans won.

The '94 election signified a loss of the old faith in government. But Americans still don't understand the full implications of rejecting the legacy of FDR, JFK, LBJ, Nixon, Carter, and Clinton. They still don't understand that they're going to have to wean themselves from the teat of government and live within their means. They aren't yet ready to give up their welfare bene-

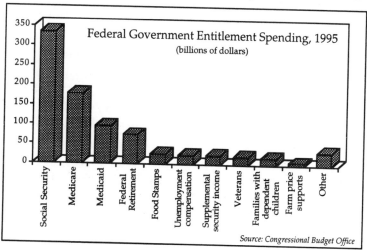

Federal Government Entitlement Spending, 1995
(billions of dollars)

Source: *Congressional Budget Office*

fits, but they do understand that something is fundamentally wrong, and that if they continue to expand the power of government, their quality of life will continue to deteriorate.

The Republicans understand this evasion. That's why their "Contract With America" promised tax cuts and a balanced budget *and* promised to keep the biggest entitlement programs intact and to increase defense spending. The Republicans have fudged the math, pretending that the economy will be stimulated so much by their tax cuts that personal income will rise to the point where taxes, even at their lower rates, would cover the shortfall.

This is so idiotic that hardly any Republicans actually believe it. It is simply impossible to increase military spending, cut taxes by $50 billion per year, and eliminate a $200 billion deficit without touching the $885 billion of entitlements. But Americans were not yet ready to face reality, so not a single Republican congressional candidate could summon the courage to admit that Congress cannot cut taxes without increasing the deficit or cutting such popular programs as Social Security and Medicare. The Contract With America is fundamentally dishonest.

Yet the dishonesty of the Contract With America pales beside the dishonesty of the Democratic alternative. "All politics is local," House Speaker Tip O'Neill used to say. What O'Neill (and the Democrats who like to quote him) meant was that you can increase government power and taxes in Washington, D.C., then go home to your district and tell the voters that you are working to cut taxes and regulation. If you deliver enough pork, answer constituents' letters promptly, and don't get caught with your hand in the cookie jar, your district will re-elect you forever. So Democrats ran for office with no program at all, just vague sloganeering about "moving forward."

Of course, the Republicans do advocate cutting some entitlements — just not for their middle-class constituents. Look at the chart below. It details entitlement spending for 1995. This is all so-called "off-budget" spending; that is, it will be spent without

Congress having to approve it.

Note that of the $885 billion spent on federal entitlements in 1995, only $140 billion goes to the poor (and their middle-class social workers). The rest goes to programs that primarily benefit the "forgotten" middle class: Medicare, college loans, federal retirement benefits, Social Security, veterans' benefits, etc.

These entitlement programs amount to over half of all federal spending. Together with interest on the national debt (which is also spent whether Congress authorizes it or not), in less than a decade they will consume more than 75% of all federal spending. At that point, the pressure for even higher taxes and the consequent decline in productivity will likely lead to an economic crisis. And like past economic crises, the ultimate result will probably be a tremendous increase in state power.

But neither the Republicans nor the Democrats will cut entitlements for the middle class. This is one thing you can bet on. The Democrats designed the programs and have always supported them. The Republicans are sometimes a little bit critical, but they don't want to risk losing votes by supporting cuts. During the Reagan administration, spending on entitlements rose substantially, despite Reagan's rhetoric against them.

There is one exception. In California, Republican Governor Pete Wilson faced a budget crisis. He was afraid even to stand up to the state's teachers (who are politically organized and view their outrageous salaries as an entitlement), let alone the beneficiaries of the state's "generous" welfare system. So he raised taxes and watched his voter approval ratings collapse. Then he discovered an entitlement he could oppose: government aid to illegal immigrants, the one group of people who live in California but cannot vote.

Of course, Wilson didn't suggest that since illegal immigrants can't get the emoluments to which their fellow Californians are entitled, they should be exempt from taxes. He prefers to collect their money and show them the back of his hand. Capitalizing on the issue, he rose from 20 points behind to an easy victory.

In mid-December of 1994, the federal government's Bipartisan Committee on Entitlement and Tax Reform finished its investigations. The 32-member commission quickly identified the problem, and developed 52 different proposals to bring entitlement spending under control. The result was an orgy of complaint from the recipients. And there are a lot of recipients: the *average* American family receives more than $10,000 per year from Uncle Sam.

In a show of courage typical of American politicians, the Commission never even voted on whether to endorse any of the proposed cuts. In the end, it decided not even to issue a report. Instead, it sent a letter to President Clinton ominously warning that "tough action is needed sooner rather than later."

So this is where we are today. Most Americans have come to realize that the tax and tax, spend and spend, elect and elect philosophy of the Democrats isn't working. They realize that changes have to be made, and they are willing to turn to the Republicans. But so far, the Republicans have lacked the will to provide real leadership, to make the hard decisions to cut middle-class entitlements. (After controlling Congress for barely a week, GOP leaders had already backed down on cutting the pork from the Small Business Administration, on reducing farm subsidies — even on their promise to sell off a surplus House of Representatives office building. By 1996, when House Budget Committee Chair John Kasich was pressed to name some programs that had actually been cut, he managed to come up with only one: a tick eradication program in Puerto Rico.)

The 1994 election gave the Republicans an opportunity similar to the one handed the Democrats in 1930. If they can come up with a vision for the future and a coherent program for its implementation, they can become a long-term majority party. If they fail, they will be dumped into the ashcan of history, and the voters will elect a new party that can provide a coherent program.

But whatever happens in the next few years, one thing is certain: the political theory that has dominated the twentieth century so powerfully that it was advocated by almost all politicians, whether Democratic or Republican, is dead. The 1994 election was a crisis of faith. Americans realized, for a moment at least, that we cannot spend money we do not have, that we cannot take money from ourselves and spread it around and make ourselves better off.

Whether Americans will emerge from this crisis with a new, *Republican* faith in government as miracle-worker — one that can solve the problem of the breakdown of the family by throwing money at it, the problem of drug abuse by arresting marijuana smokers, the problem of crime by hiring more policemen and giving mandatory life sentences to people caught with foreign bank accounts — remains to be seen.

The alternative is to dispense with faith in government altogether, to return to the older view of government as a human institution bound by the same natural laws as the ecosystem and the same economic laws as society itself, and to realize that a system in which individual liberty is maximized will optimize human beings' ability to flourish. There is substantial rhetorical support for this view. In a press conference the day after the election, Sen. Phil Gramm told reporters:

> It is not going to be easy to reverse 40 years of government policy. It is not going to be easy to reform a program like welfare. It is not going to be easy to ask and demand that the 40 million people riding in the wagon get out of the wagon and help the rest of us pull it. But it's something that has to be done if we're going to save our country. The American people are for it. They have given us the mandate to do it. They have sent us eleven new Republicans who are going to come into Washington like Teddy Roosevelt's Rough Riders, and they are not going to be of a mind to cut some type of a deal with Bill Clinton to raise taxes half as much, to increase spending half as much, and to implement half as many new government regulations. They are going to be coming to Washington to reverse

that process, to cut government spending, to reduce regulations, to let working people keep more of what they earn.

Those are powerful words. But we've heard powerful words before, only to see those who spoke powerfully compromise and the government continue to grow. Gramm seemed aware of this danger:

I am willing to compromise with the president as long as we're moving in the right direction. If we're talking about compromise where we meet the president halfway in moving in the right direction, that's a compromise that I'm willing to consider. But I am not willing to compromise meeting the president halfway and going in the wrong direction. Why should we want to go halfway in the wrong direction?

Gramm himself has had trouble living up to these words. He has never been one to shy away from porkbarrel programs that benefit his constituencies — he fought hard to bring the superconductor project to Texas, backed the government-created Sematech consortium, and even voted for the mohair wool subsidy — and has expressed ultra-statist views on the topics of crime control and drugs. But he did not become the Republican presidential nominee in 1996, and neither did anyone else who might be perceived, rightly or wrongly, as a challenge to the dying status quo. Instead, the GOP chose Bob Dole, a man who has spent more than half his life as an elected politician. In over 35 years in Congress, Dole helped engineer virtually every program of the big-government paradigm. As Newt Gingrich put it, Dole is "the tax collector for the welfare state."

If the election were to be decided on issues and personalities alone, Clinton would be a shoo-in. Given the choice between a young, energetic opportunist and a tired old man who spent most of his life building leviathan, I think the voters will go for youth.

But there is a reasonable possibility that the election will not be decided on the basis of issues and personalities. Although much of the public has remained indifferent to the evidence that the Clintons were part of a massive scheme to defraud the tax-payers, the media and the Republicans have not. Criminal and legislative investigations are proceeding against the Clintons. If a "smoking gun" proving the Clintons' guilt is found, Dole may win. But short of such conclusive and obvious evidence, Clinton may very well be re-elected.

This is not to say that the evidence against the Clintons isn't very strong. In fact, the evidence of their guilt is powerful. But the criminal activity they engage is also very complicated, and Americans are not exactly anxious to learn that the man they elected president is a common criminal.

The Clintons are two Yale-trained attorneys perpetrating complex white-collar crimes, covering their tracks using all the sophisticated tricks that they and their coterie of even more high-powered shysters can muster. The Clintons' schemes were put together by slick lawyers with an eye toward making them difficult to detect; Bill and Hillary have "lost" important documents, and lied about various facts when questioned by the press.

The Clintons have yet to testify before Congress on the Whitewater affair. But Mrs. Clinton has testified about another small matter: her preemptory firing and prosecution of the White House travel office staff and hiring her cronies to take its place. On March 21, Hillary Clinton responded in writing to a series of Congressional questions about the "Travelgate" mess. Here is a box score of her answers (*Wall Street Journal*, April 9):

"I do not recall"/"I cannot recall"	21
"I do not believe"	9
"I have no knowledge"/"I have no first-hand knowledge"/"I have no personal knowledge"	7
"I simply don't know"/"I don't know"/ "I do not know how"/"I do not know what"	5
"It is possible"/"It is quite possible that I had"/ "It is possible that I may have"	4
"I believe"	3
"I may have spoken"	3
"I have no specific recollection"	2

"I may have expressed the view"	2
"I cannot identify"	2
"I do not know for certain"/"I do not know how"	1
"It is hard to remember"	1
"I have tried to state . . . such recollection as I have"	1
"It is . . . difficult now to distinguish"	1
"I believe I became aware"	1
"I do not remember precisely"	1
"I have a vague recollection"	1
"I am not aware"	1
"He may have mentioned"	1

In all, some 67 lapses of memory about a series of events that occurred less than three years earlier.

Will this sort of obfuscation, in combination with convenient loss of documentary evidence and feckless defense by Clinton's partisans manage to fend on the investigators, at least until the election? This is the question upon which the election hangs.

But in the long run, its answer will make no more difference on the direction of American public life than the wind blowing up the Columbia River gorge makes on the flow of that great river. If Clinton manages to be re-elected, it remains overwhelmingly unlikely that another Democrat will follow him to the White House. The old political faith has lost its appeal.

And the Democratic Party will not be able to change its approach: it is beholden to too many interest groups whose prosperity and in some cases very existence depends on the old ways. Indeed, if Clinton is re-elected, he is unlikely to complete his second term. The ever-growing weight of evidence of his involvement in the Whitewater fraud will eventually be too much for his presidency to bear. His personal denoument will be the same whether he is re-elected or not: ignominy. His public career will likely end with a presidential pardon, either from President Gore or President Dole. Gore would pardon him as an act of fealty, Dole to avoid the appearance of hypocrisy. (He supported Ford's pardon of Nixon in 1973.) But all these are minor details in comparison to the great drama playing itself out on our national stage. The old political religon is on its death bed. The road we have been traveling is the road to economic decline, tyrannical government controls, and increasing public corruption.

Whether the American citizen is ready to face reality, to accept the fact that government can only spend resources that it takes from its citizens, and to understand that the price of higher taxes and more intrusive regulation is economic stagnation remains to be seen.

If the Republicans or some new party can find the courage and the intelligence to articulate to the American people that the way to return to a prosperous, free, and open society is to return to the principles of self-reliance and individual responsibility by cutting spending, cutting taxes, eliminating regulations, restoring civil liberties, and re-establishing property rights, then the future of our country can be greater than its past.

But if no one finds that vision, if no one has the necessary courage, if no one articulates the policies that are needed, then the U.S. can look forward to a lengthy decline of the sort that turned Britain from the wealthiest nation on Earth at the beginning of this century to the poverty-laden welfare state it is today.

Contributors

Chester Alan Arthur is *Liberty*'s political correspondent.

Caroline Baum is an online columnist for Dow Jones Telerate.

R.W. Bradford is editor and publisher of *Liberty*.

Douglas Casey is editor of *Crisis Investing* newsletter and author of several books, including *Crisis Investing for the Rest of the '90s*.

Stephen Cox is author of *Love and Logic: The Evolution of Blake's Thought*.

Richard D. Fisher is secretary and treasurer of the Arizona chapter of the Association of American Physicians and Surgeons.

Leon T. Hadar is a Washington-based journalist whose work appears in U.S. and foreign publications.

Victor Niederhoffer is a commodities trader and merchant banker.

Randal O'Toole is editor of *Different Drummer* and president of the Thoreau Institute.

Fred L. Smith, Jr. is president of the Competitive Enterprise Institute.